"THE HIGHER CHRISTIAN LIFE"

SOURCES FOR THE STUDY OF THE HOLINESS, PENTECOSTAL, AND KESWICK MOVEMENTS

*A forty-eight-volume facsimile
series reprinting extremely
rare documents for the study of
nineteenth-century religious
and social history, the rise
of feminism, and the
history of the Pentecostal and
Charismatic movements*

Edited by

Donald W. Dayton
Northern Baptist Theological Seminary

Advisory Editors

D. William Faupel, *Asbury Theological Seminary*
Cecil M. Robeck, Jr., *Fuller Theological Seminary*
Gerald T. Sheppard, *Union Theological Seminary*

A GARLAND SERIES

MIRACLES IN THE SLUMS

Seth Cook Rees

Garland Publishing, Inc.
New York & London
1985

For a complete list of the titles in this series
see the final pages of this volume.

Library of Congress Cataloging in Publication Data

Rees, Seth Cook.
MIRACLES IN THE SLUMS.

("The Higher Christian life")
Reprint. Originally published: Chicago :
S.C. Rees, [1905].
1. Church and social problems—Illinois—Chicago.
2. City missions—Illinois—Chicago.   3. Holiness
churches—Missions—Illinois—Chicago.   4. Church work
with prostitutes—Illinois—Chicago.   I. Title.
II. Series.
HN80.C5R44   1985   261.8'3'0977311   84-24746
ISBN 0-8240-6440-2 (alk. paper)

The volumes in this series are printed on
acid-free, 250-year-life paper.

Printed in the United States of America

Yours & His
Seth C. Rees.

Miracles in the Slums

OR

THRILLING STORIES

Of Those Rescued from the Cesspools of Iniquity, and Touching Incidents in the Lives of the Unfortunate

By SETH COOK REES

Author of "The Ideal Pentecostal Church," "Fire from Heaven," and the "Holy War."

"He hath sent me to bind up the broken-hearted, to proclaim liberty to the captives, and the opening of the prison to them that are bound." Isaiah 61 : 1.

SETH COOK REES, PUBLISHER
533 North Pine Avenue
CHICAGO

DEDICATION.

To three hundred and fifty thousand of my fallen sisters in America: to three million homeless, friendless, tramping men: to one hundred thousand men and boys in penitentiaries, workhouses, and jails: to one hundred thousand newsboys: to one hundred thousand bootblacks: to the sick, destitute, and unfortunate everywhere, is this book tenderly dedicated, with the Christian love of the author.

May 20, 1905.

PREFACE.

As the time has come to send forth this book to the reading public, I have a very keen sense of the fact that it but faintly portrays the awful situation as found in our great centers of population. While some of our statements will be regarded by many as extravagant, and our word-pictures as overdrawn, yet as I think of it now, I have a deep and growing conviction that in our setting forth these pages we have not approximated a fair description of the real state of things as they exist to-day.

There are some things that can not be exaggerated. No newspaper reporter has ever yet been able in his description to overdraw a real cyclone, and if you have ever been in one, you are quite ready to agree with me. The slime, squalor, and crime of our slimiest slums baffles all power of description; in fact, we would not, if we could, attempt to describe much that we have found of unnameable sin, shame, and crime.

For more than a quarter of a century I have at times been greatly burdened for the neglected, fallen, and poverty-stricken of this world. When but a youth I was often melted to tears and moved to deep feelings of compassion in reading the stories of London's poor, or the street urchins of our great American cities. In all these years the story of a fallen woman has simply broken my heart, but I never imagined that God would ever honor me with the glorious privilege of being connected in any small way with a movement for the accomplishment of such an exalted work.

My primary object in setting forth these pages is the honor of God by showing positively, and with emphasis, the power of Christ to save the lowest of the low, to renew the most ruined and wrecked lives, and revive and restore the most blasted hopes.

Second, to reach the unreached, unwashed, and unchurched, and lead them to the Christ who has wrought such marvelous transformation in the lives of those whose history is given here.

Third, to give an incentive to the faith and holy activity of good people everywhere, many of whom have never been sufficiently aroused to the sense of the magnitude of sin, or the possibilities of grace. I sincerely pray Almighty God, in the name of Jesus Christ, His Son, and my Saviour, to use this book as a means to this end. Ten thousand blessings upon all who read these pages.

SETH COOK REES.

TABLE OF CONTENTS.

LIST OF ILLUSTRATIONS.

MRS. S. C. REES, OUR FIRST SLUM MISSIONARY.

A MARKET FOR GIRLS.

WE are often confronted by those who persist in discrediting and denying the existence of a well-organized commercial trade in girls in this country. But as certainly as cattle and hogs are bought and sold in the stockyards in Chicago, so certainly are thousands of pure, artless, innocent girls procured from every State in the Union and sold in the market in " Custom House Place," " Little Hell," " Black Lane," " Tenderloin District," or some such precincts of sin. These commercial devils of both sexes as really own and hold the girls in their possession as any Southern slaveholder ever controlled the negroes owned by him.

These poor girls are behind closed doors of shame, and walls thicker than any penitentiary walls. Held in bondage to the brutal passions of beastly men, their slavery is more infernal than any slavery of this or any other country.

Hundreds of these American daughters are incarcerated where their sobs and groans are never heeded, and their midnight cries are never heard. The public seemed temporarily shocked when three of these pure country girls who had been allured from Canadian homes, were recovered from one of these haunts of shame, in Chicago, and returned to their parents and native homes.

They were induced to leave home under the promise of easy employment and large pay, never dreaming they were as lambs going to their slaughter. At the depot they were met and ushered into a closed carriage, driven to a certain number in a certain street; the door opened, they were ushered in, the door closed. Alas! they were in the vestibule of hell. Placed in an inner court, their screams and cries could not be heard to the street. Robbed of their virtue, they were ruined for life, and for two long weeks suffered untold torture.

Eternity alone can reveal the agony and horror of those awful days, and " awfuller " nights. At the end of two strange, black weeks, days so rayless, and nights so starless, that to these pure country girls it seemed like hell itself, a little colored girl who scrubbed the front steps dropped a word to a passing policeman, and the chief sent a posse of officers with shotguns, and the enslaved daughters were rescued and returned to their distracted parents.

But they were *ruined,* their names were *tarnished,* their lives *withered, blighted,* and *damned,* and it is not likely that the commercial agent received more than seventy-five dollars for

the three of them. We have never found a higher
market for the most attractive and desirable than
thirty dollars a head. Many of our girls who are
now wonderfully saved were sold in the market
for five dollars, and some of them went as low as
two dollars a head.

Mother, what value do you place upon your
daughter? *You* probably value her very highly,
but she has another value — a commercial value,
in this commercial world, and it is probably somewhere from five to twenty-five dollars. If she has
a fine form, a beautiful face, and is in every way
attractive, and should be put on a bullish market,
she might bring twenty-five or thirty dollars; but
if she is an ordinary girl, no difference how much
you love her, she will not bring as much if sold by
the pound as well-fatted hogs are worth in the
Union Stockyards of Chicago. This is the value
placed on your darling by this licentious rum-
soaked world. I am not dealing in sentimental-
ism. I am not pessimistic, and yet I pity the man
who feels forced to be an optimist in these days
of thickening gloom.

I am dealing with *great, rugged, bald, craggy
facts,*— bare hard facts that you had just as well
face. In one of the most popular American cities
we found a liquor dealer with his stock pens in the

same building where his saloon was situated. The market pen was screened off with lattice from the floor to the ceiling, or so high that escape was impossible. The girls were turned into that enclosure, and men looked them over through that wire screen and made their choice just as they would select any other article of merchandise.

One of our Chicago missionaries has finally succeeded in one of the most difficult undertakings of gaining admittance into a Japanese sporting house, or a house where only Japanese girls are kept. The most beautiful and innocent-looking Japanese girls that can be found in the empire are bought and shipped to this country for such purposes of cruelty and shame. The house, while it is kept by an American woman, is after the Japanese style, and in elegance and splendor, baffles description. The house is patronized only by wealthy, aristocratic, American men. The girls are all small and, dressed in the finest silks, they look like beautiful dolls. Think of their heartaches and sorrows — strangers among strangers. The same infernal commercial business is carried on by shipping our American girls in droves to the foreign lands to receive the same treatment. One of our friends, a missionary in Bombay, India, was notified that on a certain steamer there were twenty-six American girls, who had been shipped under promise of employment with a certain great corporation, with good pay, but that they were shipped to an agent for the sporting market. The missionary, as well as the agent, was on the lookout for them. But the vessel came a day earlier than the agent expected, and he was not at the wharf. The missionary was there, and when those twenty-six girls stood on the wharf, and were informed what they were in India for, they wept and sobbed, and even screamed aloud. Thank God! she had a place to take them to, and rescued them all from ruin. But it breaks our hearts to think of the thousands who are less fortunate. One of the most adroit methods used in this fiendish merchandise of souls is the "mock marriage." Elegantly dressed demons in human form, gallant in manners, attentive to a fault, with the most deceptive words, gain the confidence, then the affections, of the most innocent and artless of American daughters.

Mock licenses are obtained, the services of a mock preacher are secured, and the parsonage proves to be a house of ill fame, and this introduces my first story — the relation of which is intended to riot only glorify God, and magnify the grace of His dear Son, but to warn parents and daughters

2

everywhere, for this dark misfortune comes not only to those in the ordinary walks of life, but to the palatial homes, boulevards, and avenues.

LITTLE MAY.

"LITTLE MAY."

A COMMERCIAL agent traveling in the interest of one of the well-known houses of shame in Cincinnati, was making a business trip through the South. He approached a certain town, registered in a good hotel, and started out in search of victims.

As soon as his eyes fell upon the attractive form and beautiful face of " Little May," he began laying plans for her ruin. He had made a study of human nature, and saw in her a fine specimen of womanhood. He promptly embraced what he knew to be a rare opportunity. He was most careful of all his movements. At first his point was merely to meet her every few days, and every time so polite as to soon make her feel she was somewhat acquainted with him, and then when received into her home it was always in the presence of her parents. He so completely covered his tracks that nothing appeared out of the way.

He secured her confidence, won her affections, and in a short time proposed marriage. It seemed impossible for her to decline the offer. Her parents were Christians, and had strange impressions about it all, but seemed unable to dissuade her from her purpose. The villain had completely captured her affectionate nature; she loved him, and would go with him to the ends of the earth. Having succeeded thus far, he gave plausible reasons why they should be married in Cincinnati.

To this her parents stoutly objected, but to no purpose. When in Cincinnati, a license was secured (she supposed it was a license), and they went to the " parsonage " (?) (she was told it was a parsonage), where they would be joined in a happy union. She was only seventeen, and her young, confiding heart was full of hope. When the parsonage (?) door was opened and they were ushered in, she found herself amid strange surroundings. Very soon her supposed husband excused himself with the promise that he would return soon.

Little May was overwhelmed by the strange actions about her, and when her supposed husband's return seemed delayed, there came a great lump in her throat, and with streaming eyes, and a forlorn look, she sat there one of the purest of girls amid the vilest of earth. But, oh! who can imagine her feelings when the madam told her he would never return — that she had just paid him thirty dollars for her.

Her anguish and grief seemed too much for any

human frame. No pen can describe it — it can never be expressed. She was only told that it was not worth while to weep, that it was an easy way of making money, and she would soon overcome those feelings.

Little do fathers and mothers think as their little brood gather about the evening fireside in the childish glee of a happy home, that such a fate should ever come to them. But, alas! the plunderer's hand is abroad—the destroyer is in the land! It was two or three months before Little May's escape was possible. One day one of our faithful missionaries forced an entrance into that haunt of vice, and Little May was recovered and brought to one of our Rescue Homes.

It was not long till she was wonderfully saved from all sin, and after a short time we returned her to her heart-broken parents in the South. They had wept and prayed and cried to God day and night for some clue to their precious darling who seemed lost to them forever.

Can you imagine their joy when she re-entered the old home and rested her throbbing head just where it used to rest on her mother's breast? When her father planted kiss after kiss just where he used to plant them in her childhood days? You ask if rescue work pays? Beloved, if Little

May had been my daughter, don't you suppose I would think it pays? If May had been *your* daughter, would you have ever asked the question?

I am often asked what per cent of the girls rescued really get saved, and stand true. I have just had a report from one of our Homes which includes an answer to that question. It is, that eighty-five per cent of all who have come into that Home have proved true. Where is an evangelist that can show such proportionate results in churches? Who can show sixty per cent, forty per cent, or ten per cent, of their converts at the end of a year? Jesus always thought it would pay to save the fallen, and I know of no investment equal to it anywhere. To Him be all the glory for the power of the Gospel in the slums.

A NATION'S SHAME.

"I AM not ashamed of the Gospel of Christ."
There is much to be ashamed of in these days, both
in the Church and State. The Church should be
ashamed that she is utterly failing to evangelize
the world. While all Christendom made three
million professed converts to Christianity, in the
foreign field the heathen increased two hundred
million. In the face of this fact she should be
ashamed to listen to her high salaried, ease-loving,
time serving preachers, announcing that the world
is getting better, and that we are approaching a
millennium of righteousness. She should be
ashamed of her tall steeples, thundering organs,
thick carpets, and salaried singers, with no converts. She should be ashamed that her church
fairs, festivals, bazaars, and shows are thronged
with people, and the prayer-meeting can hardly be
sustained. At a little country Quaker church, there
were fifty to the social one night, and only one to
the prayer-meeting the next. My information
leads me to believe that this is a common proportion in Protestantism.

The State should be ashamed of the hundreds
of ship loads of distilled damnation she is shipping

into the ports of less enlightened nations, to wreck their homes, widow their wives, make orphans of their children, and damn their souls in an eternal hell. This government should be ashamed that in the very heart of the nation, there are three million mountaineers, who are most of them unable to either read or write, and are practically without the Gospel of Christ.

She has three million homeless, friendless, tramping men. Most of people fear and dread them, and no one scarcely loves them. You may have given some of them a sandwich at the back door to get rid of them, but who invites them in and points them to Jesus? Who gets them on their knees for prayer? There are a hundred thousand newsboys and one hundred thousand bootblacks, but few of them have ever been prayed for by name. Who knows their names? Many of them have no name except " Dick," " Tut," " Jim," " Bob," " Toad," or " Jack." Many of them sleep in goods' boxes, cellar ways, box-cars, or dark alleys. Nobody to tuck them in, and no one to say " good-night."

There are a hundred thousand men and boys in penitentiaries, workhouses and jails, who are there on account of a legalized traffic in wholesale dam- nation. This infernal trade is not only made possible by the ballot of the American people, but receives the sanction of a so-called Christian nation.

But worst of all there are three hundred and fifty thousand of most beautiful American girls behind sealed doors and walls thicker than any penitentiary walls — slaves to the brutal passions of beastly men. Their sobs, groans, and midnight cries are unheeded, and their sorrow is unknown to the world. This should certainly make a nation blush with shame, and send the Christian church to her knees with prayers and tears.

Thank God for something of which we are never ashamed. It is the Gospel of Christ — a gospel for the poor, the fallen, and the hopeless, and if you read this book, you will not wonder at its title, or at our convictions.

ORPHA.

ORPHA, THE CIGARETTE FIEND.

IT would seem that God is going out of His way, in these last days, to lift up and save poor, lost, wrecked, and ruined lives. He has always loved the fallen, but the truly observing can hardly fail to notice that the Holy Ghost is giving special attention to the neglected and submerged classes. It would be wise as well as pious for us to give more attention to those to whom the Lord is showing special attention.

Christ was a traveling Saviour; He journeyed from city to city, from village to village and from hamlet to hamlet. When He was rejected at one place, He went to another; and He commanded His followers to do the same. He is just the same to-day. Educational and ecclesiastical seminaries of the world have had their opportunity and in the early part of the last century great revivals of Bible salvation broke out in many of the colleges and universities of America; and many of the churches enjoyed great out-pourings of grace, but having been rejected and often insulted, the blessed Spirit seems to have gone outside of the city walls, under the hedges, through the valleys, and to the grimy lanes of life to seek the fallen, and they seem much more anxious to have Him than those Scribes and Pharisees or doctors of the law.

Orpha, the subject of this sketch, was born in Ohio. Her father was a wicked man; her mother, a godly, praying woman, went to heaven when Orpha was fifteen years old — just at the time when she most needed the protection and counsel of a mother. A stepmother soon turned her father against his children and the poor girl was homeless. She worked in a shoe factory, the pay was not large and she had a hard time.

O, how my heart breaks over the thousands of friendless girls in mills, shops, and cotton factories, struggling for food and clothes and exposed to awful temptation to sin and ruin! These girls feel keenly the need of some one to love and care for them. Thousands of women are bestowing their affections on a poodle dog or a sleepy old cat, who ought to rise up and take these girls into their homes and hearts.

Orpha's first break into sin was not until she was twenty years old and then under promise of marriage. How shall the daughters of our land be warned against the scoundrels who with good clothes and fair promises are ruining whole regiments of girls? When deserted by the one who had sworn to support her, there seemed nothing to open before her but a life of shame. She went to church, but they did not have salvation to save her; the saloon and brothel were wide open to her. A well-dressed man, a demon in human form, came to the country village and under promise of good clothes and a nice home with light work, he allured the tired girl to Cincinnati and sold her to a house of shame. Her cries and groans were unanswered; she was lost to the world and womanhood and there was nobody to care. The man was a professional procurer, and in this case received only two dollars each for the girls above their traveling expenses.

Mother, how much is your daughter worth? Have you a daughter under twenty years of age? Would you sell her for two dollars? Father, what do you think of a man who would allure your daughter away, and then sell her for two dollars to be a slave to the brutal passions of beastly men? The sweet, pure child who has climbed into your lap, and fondly stroked your whiskers so many times; perhaps she is sitting on your knee while you read this sketch; she may yet be exposed to this hellish scheme. There are hundreds of men abroad in the land to-day whose business is to procure pure, handsome country or village girls for sporting houses of our great cities. I can not write

this sketch without uttering a warning against this
infernal traffic.

This slave-driver, the villain that he was, told
Orpha afterward that he would give anything in
the world if he had never brought her to this place
of shame; withered, blighted, paralyzed as his soul
was, it still seemed awful to him to see her in that
horrid bondage where her midnight cries were
never answered and where there was not a ray of
hope of escaping. How then, must it seem to a
pure, sensitive nature? When all was lost, she
went lower and lower, smoking and drinking until
she was a perfect sot. From one sporting house to
a lower class house and to another and another,
down and down until she often wished she was
dead and really felt that hell could be no worse.
She secured a revolver and was just about to kill
herself when some one learned of the plan and
broke down the door of her room and took the gun
from her just in time to save her life.

It was in this forlorn, hopeless condition that a
voice spoke to her in the night and said, " Get up
and pray, there is coming a change in your life."
The voice was so plain and so oft repeated that she
obeyed, and while she did not know how to pray or
how to get salvation, from that hour she was seized

with conviction and could never get rid of it; and although she was not converted, the conviction was so strong that she quit smoking and the desire for cigarettes was all taken away. She told the madam of the house that she could not smoke any more, and although she did not quit sin and, of course, was not converted, she would weep by the hour and talk about Jesus in the brothel and many times would get down and pray right among the girls and with the keeper of the house, and they would weep with her, but they did not know how to get saved. Then she would drink and drink for weeks and drown her conviction and as soon as she would sober off, she would pray and weep and preach Jesus to those in the house, until the conviction was so great that they told her she would have to leave if she did not stop it, but she could not stop and they could do nothing with her.

She was arrested eight times in the month of April, and served five weeks in the workhouse and all this time she was weeping and praying and struggling to find the light of God.

When she heard music which reminded her of her mother and her mother's warnings, she would weep and weep, and almost went wild. Again she attempted suicide, but her plans were thwarted,

3

and she was brought to Hope Cottage, where she heard that Jesus could save her from all sin, and keep her true to God always.

As soon as she was told how, the poor, tired, heart-broken girl gave her heart to God, and He wonderfully saved her from sin, and all desire for sin. Her conversion was so wonderful that she declared that she was sanctified wholly, and would listen to nothing else, until God showed her inbred sin, and then she sought with all her heart the second blessing, and was sanctified wholly. She feels called to do mission work among those of her own kind. Before she was saved, she would not work; now she is delighted to engage in honest labor; will wash and iron all day, and give of her means to spread the Gospel. She says, " I am free from all passions and sinful desires: I am settled and esablished, and no one can make me doubt it. If all the sanctified people were to go back on the Lord, I know He has sanctified me, and I want to do missionary work for Him."

Orpha has since been ordained as a deaconess, and is one among our most successful missionaries. Again and again she has stood like a princess in the same court room, and before the same Judge, where her ragged form was dragged from the cell before the bench, morning after morning; but now she stands there dressed like a Christian lady, pleading for the release of other girls, and commanding the profoundest respect of the court, and of the officers who so often secured her arrest. One day she entered the court, dressed in a handsome black suit, with white collar and cuffs, as you see her in this picture. The judge rose to his feet, invited her forward, and when he and the officers had taken her by the hand in congratulation, said. " Georgia (for that was her sporting name), we are all very glad indeed of your reformation." Immediately Orpha turned on him and said, " Judge, I want you to know it is not reformation, but salvation through Jesus Christ." She has since rescued many poor girls, among them Fannie, whose story is found in this book. She is also the missionary referred to in the article, " Judgment in the Slums." The following is a clipping from a newspaper: —

BEGS FOR CHANCE TO REFORM SHOPLIFTER.

WOMAN MISSIONARY, ONCE PRISONER IN POLICE STATION, PLEADS TO SAVE YOUNG GIRL.

CINCINNATI, JAN. 7.—A sensation was created in police court circles yesterday by the reappearance of Georgia Kline, who came in the interest of Lauretta Daul, of Trenton, N. J., a nineteen-year-old girl, who confessed to Chief Crawford that she had been for months shoplifting. A few months ago Georgia Kline was a physical and moral wreck. Addicted to liquor and drugs, her ragged form was dragged from the cell to the rail before the bench, morning after morning. Yesterday her appearance was a revelation of reform. Dressed in a handsome tailor-made suit of broadcloth, black from toe to crown, and heavily veiled, she was a picture of prosperity and decorum. " I am a missionary now, Judge; let me have that little girl; let me take her to my new home, and we, I and those who have helped me, will reform her." Judge Leuders promptly gave Lauretta Daul over to the applicant.

Beloved, it is " the gospel which is the power of God unto salvation," that has done this. To Him we give all the honor and glory forever. Beloved, when I know that forty-six thousand of such girls are captured every year, is it any wonder that I ask your prayers, and in every way your assistance to rescue these for the Lord? Orpha is a good preacher of the Word, and a real soul winner, as trusty and trusted as an old veteran of the Cross. Her shining face is a living testimony to the power of the gospel, and a constant rebuke to sin. Let all who read these lines distinctly understand that we are careful to give all the glory to the Father, Son, and Holy Ghost. Praise the Lord!

A NIGHT IN "LITTLE HELL."

" LITTLE HELL " is one of the darkest sections of Chicago, North Side, and noted more for murders and robberies than for houses of prostitution, though every conceivable form of sin abounds there. The streets are narrow, dark, filthy, and abound with dirty, ragged children.

Just at dark one wet, cold night, one of our missionaries received a message asking her to take two other missionaries and go to a certain street and number in this benighted district to care for a man who was dying with delirium tremens. They were warned that it was not at all safe for them to enter that precinct at night, but feeling that the Lord would have them respond to the call, without the least hesitation proceeded on their journey. The rain was falling, the night was dismal, and the distance was several miles. When they reached the doomed neighborhood, a horror of darkness and spiritual depression settled down on their souls, and it seemed as if brimstone was in the air, and regiments of devils confronted them.

These girls, naturally as timid and shrinking as children, pressed their way through a long dark street, then turned into a darker, grimy lane, and after a lengthy journey, wet and cold, they found the slummy little house surrounded with dilapidation, presenting just such an appearance as you would expect to find around a drunkard's home.

They were received by the drunkard's heart-broken wife into a little room, with a bed, an old lounge, a small table, and some chairs. The only light was by a dingy little lamp with a smoky chimney. On the bed was a man supposed to be dying with tremens. For six weeks he had not slept an hour. His groans, screams, and delirium had worn everybody out who had been with him. Some of his worthless neighbors had been in, but would not stay. Money will do almost anything, but one thing it will not do, it will not hire people to stay and see a man die with delirium tremens, and listen to his unearthly screams when devils are after him, and snakes crawling all over him. No one seems to want money bad enough to endure this. But the grace of God will operate when everything else has failed.

The girls told the poor tired woman that she might go to bed; that there were three of them, and they were not afraid, promising that if he grew worse they would call her. Very soon the man rose right up in bed, as thin as a ghost. With eyes like a flame of fire, he screamed, *"Snakes! Snakes!"* Pointing at the wall, first in one direction, then another, he would cry, *"Can't you see the snakes? The room is full of devils."* The missionaries would just cry, " Jesus, Jesus, blessed Jesus! " and at the mention of the name of Jesus he would fall back on his pillow and remain quiet perhaps two or three minutes, and then scream again as before. This was repeated a number of times. The man was so emaciated that he seemed only skin and bones, and yet in the strength of the demons he would jump out of bed, take the lounge in his arms, and run at the missionaries. They would just fall on their knees, and cry out, " Jesus, blessed Jesus," and he would drop the lounge and get back in bed. After these awful scenes were repeated many times, the missionaries agreed about midnight that they must get down and get complete victory for this man. God wonderfully blessed them in prayer, and while they were crying to Jesus, the devils were all cast out, and that satanic feeling left the room. Yes, the devils went out, and the angels came in, and the glory of God filled and lighted that dismal room. The man began to pray for himself, and definitely gave himself to God. While he was praying, he fell asleep with the name of Jesus on his lips, and slept like a baby for eight hours.

When that frantic lunatic woke next morning, he was like a child, and was blessedly saved and in his right mind. O, glory to the Christ that is able to cast out devils and heal the sick.

The missionaries were so blessed in their souls, and lifted above this world, they seemed to hardly touch the sidewalks. As they went home next morning they were so filled with the glory of God that they stopped wagons on the street, and preached Jesus to the drivers. They stopped men on their way to their work, and women with pitchers or buckets of beer, and warned them of the coming judgment, and preached salvation to all. That was once the devil suffered awful defeat in " Little Hell."

When the missionaries returned a week later, they found the man saved and healed, and looking for work. All glory to Jesus, at the mention of whose name the demons must flee.

DICIE.

DICIE, OR THE SPORTING MADAM!

DICIE was a madam of a well-furnished house of shame. At the age of twenty-four she was a confirmed drunkard. For six years she was a cigarette fiend, using morphine and cocaine, and in fact all the drugs commonly used by sporting women. Her beautiful, attractive face was bloated and greatly marred by every abominable excess. If we could show you a picture of her face as it was when she left sin, the contrast between the two portraits would appear very striking.

The slum missionaries entered her home and were permitted to pray in her house, and from that hour conviction for sin fell upon D—— like a stroke. She was urged to give up sin, and come to Rest Cottage, but was so firmly held in the mighty grip of appetite, passion, and habit that release seemed impossible. Some time later she came to the Home just for a day to look it over and see what the matron and missionaries were like. The saints wept, prayed, and pleaded with her, but she returned to her place of shame at night.

A few weeks later she came to the matron and said, " I am so *tired* and *sick* of *sin*. I want to

43

break up my house, bring part of my furnishings to Rest Cottage, give my heart to God, and if possible, find salvation from sin."

After a few days in the Home, much of her time spent in seeking God, she felt that before He would save her soul, she must apologize to a man in the slums, whom I have no doubt was many times worse than herself; but she felt that she had wronged him, and must make it right. She was not willing to trust herself down in town alone, so asked the matron if she could not send a missionary with her. The missionaries were all busy. The matron said, " I will send Anna with you." Anna was one of the inmates of the Home, who had been rescued, and so wonderfully saved that she was very trusty. D—— had been used to the protection of a revolver, but instead they each took a Bible under their arms as a sort of testimony, as well as protection from sin.

When she had seen the villain, and told him she had quit sin, broken up her house, and was seeking God, she exhorted him to do the same. When she had finished her errand and reached the street, she said to Anna, " There is a certain bartender in a saloon down here that I feel that I should speak to."

They entered the saloon, and after informing

him what she had done, she stood in that dirty saloon and preached Jesus to that bartender till he was put under the direst conviction. She was not yet converted herself, but warned him of a coming judgment, and exhorted him to come to God. She finally insisted that he should get down on his knees and she would pray with him on that saloon floor. She had not only given up sin, but had more concern for lost souls before she was converted at all than most of professing Christians have ever known.

The bartender insisted that it was hardly the proper place to pray. His customers were coming and going, and greatly embarrassed, he excused himself, taking from her a mission card, and promised that he would come down to the mission. Soon after the girls returned to the home, the physical and mental reaction set in with poor D——. The sudden abandonment of all drugs and nicotine proved too great a shock to her system, and she was thrown into temporary insanity. This was an awful blow to us all. For days the matron was forced to hide every knife, and the scissors, and watch her day and night. She would crawl through the coal scuttle in the basement, or in any way steal out and roll in the snow drifts to quench the burning thirst for strong drinks and cigarettes. She finally became so dangerously violent that it looked as if she would break up the Home. But the matron refused to turn her over to the authorities, who would have taken her to a padded cell. They fasted, prayed, and wept before God until the drug and tobacco devils were cast out of her, as really as they were in Bible times, and the dear girl was clothed and in her right mind. Oh, it was simply wonderful, beyond all description.

We soon learned that she had a mother living in a distant state, a beautiful Christian, who on learning of the situation, promptly came to Chicago. D——'s wonderful deliverance was before her mother reached us, and from the hour of her deliverance to this day she has never shown a trace of her insanity. Who can imagine the inexpressible joy of a Christian mother on the occasion of the return of such a prodigal daughter? They are living happily together in her mother's home, and D—— is a missionary of the Cross, seeking lost souls in the slums of her own city. Let everything that hath breath praise the Lord!

CUSTOM HOUSE PLACE.

"A SLUMMY SLUM."

It is exceedingly difficult for those living in rural districts to credit any statement that approximates a fair description of the real condition of the "slummiest slums" of our largest centers of population. We will not soon forget ourselves how we were appalled when we first came in touch with a solid block of sin, squalor, and crime, one-half mile square, located in the heart of a city of two million people.

It is safe, I think, to say it is a cube of sin, for certainly the infernal fumes from two hundred and forty-one saloons, besides brothels, dance halls, and low-grade theaters reach more than half a mile high. This dreadful precinct of sin, crime, and vice is without the restraint even of churches or Sunday-schools, and is a law unto itself. A stranger should cease to place any value upon his own life before he passes through some of the streets at high noon.

In this accompanying picture you have a view down through Custom House Place, where for block after block every single house on both sides of the street is a house of shame. It looks very quiet in the picture, but if you could see it at

4

midnight, it is filled with activity and the most glaring sin and atrocious crime.

On the following page is the picture of a single house occupied by ninety families, and but one of them known to be married. Whites and blacks promiscuously raising families without marriage. This is given as a testimony of the janitor of the building. What a field for mission work! Pray ye the Lord of the harvest to send forth more laborers into the vineyard. The gospel of Christ would transform this veritable hell into an Eden of grace, and fill it with flowers, smiles, sunshine, and purity.

A CHICAGO HOUSE OCCUPIED BY NINETY FAMILIES, BUT ONE OF THEM KNOWN TO BE MARRIED. THIS IS THE TESTIMONY OF THE JANITOR.

MARGARET.

MARGARET, THE BARREL-HOUSE SPORT.

MARGARET ——, of Canadian birth, came of godly ancestors. She was born on Owens' Sound, Ontario. Her father, an intelligent man, broke away from his religious training, and became a brute through strong drink. His devoted wife became discouraged, and entirely disheartened, and poor M—— grew wilful and disobedient. She had a great love for books, and for a time did good work in school. Her father, who was nearly always drunk, determined to keep her from securing an education, and at an early age, she was forced to go out as a servant, in a private family.

She gave good satisfaction, and a lady in Sault Ste. Marie testifies that she never had a better girl; but, alas! one of the devil's many agents won the confidence of this beautiful, artless girl, and allured her to the outskirts, and when he could accomplish his fiendish purpose in no other way, drugged, and robbed her of her womanhood. Margaret was never strong from a child, and now thinking she had committed the unpardonable sin, became heart-broken and miserable beyond description. When she returned home, it was only to be turned out in the cold and darkness by a drunken father.

How distressingly dark is the night when a ruined, heart-broken girl is thrust out and cast off by those who should guard and protect her! There was no beacon light in any direction. It was during that starless night of unbearable darkness, that a seemingly kind-hearted woman proposed that Margaret go with her where she could have a fine time and support herself without work. The unsuspecting girl so sorely in need of sympathy and kindness, was induced to go with the woman for a ride. That proved to be a long ride. The decline was alarmingly rapid. The whirling wheels of that black chariot carried her over declivities, rugged ways, and awful precipices, almost to the very gates of death and endless night. To poor Margaret it was like a stage driver going down the mountain, unable to get his foot on the brake. When she called a halt, there was nothing before her but the morgue, the potter's field, a nameless grave, and a Christless hell.

The first glass of strong drink proved that she had inherited her father's appetite for rum, and she was soon entirely beyond self-control. By the use of strong drink and cigarettes, she made a vigorous effort to stifle her conscience, never wholly at ease. The first few times she was led into saloons she called for " soft drinks," and the bartender, a demon in human clothes, would say, " You are no good if you can't drink whisky." The devil rose up in her, and she said, " I will not be behind my companions."

She fell to hard drinking, and for months was intoxicated day and night, never sober except when in jail. She said, "At first I would have times of feeling awfully bad about my life of sin, but I soon got so I did not care."

When in jail she was under awful conviction, but did not know what was the matter, or that there was a remedy. It was while she was in prison that she made up her mind to try and do better. Some one gave her a Bible and a hymn book, and she attempted to read the Bible, but the other prisoners would make all manner of sport of her; they would throw pillows, cups, or anything at her so that she could not read. She even asked the turnkey to put her in a cell alone where she could read her Bible, but no one could tell her the way of salvation. After she might have been released, she was held in the witness-cell for twenty-three days as a witness against a man who kept a house of shame.

She had become such a vicious character that
in a drunken row with a man who drew a knife
upon her, she in turn took a bottle, conquered
him, and took the knife from him. You could
hardly believe it, for she is one of the most timid,
modest, reticent girls we have ever had in the
Home, but it was the whisky devil that possessed
her. Her career in dissipation was comparatively
short, but she went with such a whirl that the
last six months of her life of sin was almost
without a sober breath. She was among that
lowest class that lounges about saloons and barrel
houses of the lowest kind.

A self-denying missionary found her in jail;
and she was soon weeping over her sins, and
through the instrumentality of the missionary she
was led to Christ there in prison, but she was
held several weeks, together with a number of
more hardened prisoners through whose influence
she lost her hope. After she was released from
prison, the missionary came with her to Rest
Cottage in Chicago, a distance of nearly six hundred miles.

Here Margaret wept her way back to the Cross,
but so terrible were her appetites and passions for
sin, that twice she broke away and went down,
but she was followed by many prayers and tears,

and one morning when one of our missionaries entered the police court in pursuit of another girl, poor Margaret sprang into her arms and said, " Sister Freeman, I have been arrested."

She had drifted into a very low house, and the house had been raided by the officers, and the madam and all the girls had been arrested. The missionary sat down by her during the session of the court. When sentence was passed, an old woman, the mother of the madam, stepped up and paid the fines for all of them. When court had adjourned and almost all had left the court room, the woman who paid the bill, which was only a dollar a head, together with the madam, stepped up to Margaret and said, " Come on now, we have paid your fine; you must go with us."

The missionary said, " No, Margaret, you don't have to go with them; you can go with me to Rest Cottage, if you like." The old woman, possessed with the devil and filled with rage, shook her fist in the missionary's face, and used language most unbecoming; her attitude was not only vicious, but apparently dangerous. But the missionary held her ground, and stood firmly at her post. Presently an officer came in, and demanded an explanation of the disturbance. When informed of the situation he turned to the

madam and her mother and said, "Get out of
here, every one of you, or I will have you arrested
again in five minutes." They lost no time in dis-
appearing, and Margaret was again brought to
Rest Cottage.

She very soon returned to the Lord, and found
an establishment in grace that she had never
known. For more than a year she has been a
successful missionary, testifying to the power of
Christ to save, leading public meetings, and turning men and women to God. When she stands in
the jail and relates to the prisoners the story of
her redemption, their hardened hearts are broken
to pieces. She has many strong and faithful
friends, and is leading a pure and beautiful life.
Again we are made to exclaim, "I am not
ashamed of the gospel of Christ, for it is the
power of God unto salvation to every one that
believeth." To Father, Son, and Holy Ghost,
be all the glory forever!

> "The day will soon be over,
>   When digging will be done —
> With no more Gems to gather,
>   So let us still press on.
> When Jesus comes to call us,
>   And says it is enough,
> The rough ones will be shining,
>   No longer in the rough."

"AMONG THE TOMBS."

It was on a Sabbath afternoon that we entered the famous Harrison Street Police Prison, to find about seventy prisoners, male and female, who were most of them arrested Saturday night, and thrown into jail to spend the Lord's day. The cells are in the basement, with but little light or ventilation, presenting the most forlorn and dismal spectacle I have ever found in any jail. The cells are about six by ten feet in size, furnished with absolutely nothing except a wooden bench on one side running the length of the cell. In one cell of this size there were eight men and boys, in another seven, and in another six, etc. An inmate in the cell where there were six, told us there *had* been eight in their cell.

Now two of these might manage in some sort of way to lie on that bench, but the other six must either stand for two nights and a day, or lie on that filthy stone floor. The only sanitary accommodations is a stream of water running through an open groove in the stone floor, across the rear end of the cells. The odor was stifling, and the vermin and squalor we do not care to describe. The prisoners' diet consists of bread and water;

the bread is served by placing a loaf the right size to fit tight between the bars. The water is in an old wooden pail, and sits on the corridor floor just outside the cell. When the prisoner wants water, he has an old rusty, oblong, tin cup which he can slip between the bars and reach the water in the pail. I am told that the great Norway rats drink out of the same pail of water, and eat off the same loaf of bread with the prisoners.

Here we found heart-broken boys in the same cells with hardened criminals. Here was just a child, the only support of his widowed mother — she standing outside the iron gate, convulsed with sorrow, and the heart-broken boy inside sobbing himself sick. He had been accused of carrying away a piece of brass from the foundry where he worked, but there was no brass in his innocent look, and no trace of crime in his childish face.

We felt that some of the officers beat the drunken, almost delirious prisoners unmercifully. An officer entered a cell and knocked a man down with his club, while we were standing at the cell door holding religious service.

It was wonderful how the power of God fell upon the place as we preached Jesus to those poor unfortunate creatures. In one ward there were perhaps twenty young men, who at first seemed hard and defiant, but their hearts melted, and they wept like rain as they all fell on their knees in prayer. Some of them professed that day to find Christ as their Saviour from sin. One beautiful girl seemed to receive the clear witness to salvation.

If the Christ of Calvary would walk through those dingy corridors, enter those grimy cells, and transform the lives of such unfortunate inmates, certainly there are no sinks or haunts of vice, where the power of the gospel is not able to save.

HALLIE.

AN ARTLESS GIRL.

HALLIE'S parents died when she was small.
No friendly hand was offered her, and the poor
child was thrown out into this cold world to be
tossed about and to make her own way. It is not
easy for a friendless, homeless child to stem the
rising tides of sin, beat back the billows of temptation, and ride on in purity with unsullied garments.

The child was taking the cows to pasture, when
a *married* man, *and a church member,* captured
and ruined her. There seemed to be no one to
care; she had never had a mother to teach her
the true sacredness of womanhood, and in her
artlessness and innocence, she was an easy prey
to this beast of the field.

When a girl has fallen, the devil almost invari-
ably says to her, " Well, you know you are ruined;
everybody will cast you off; you will be kicked
out of society; your name is tarnished, and no
body will care; you had just as well go into sin,
and get all out of life you can." Poor Hallie, like
a crippled lamb among a pack of wolves, with
aching head and breaking heart, yields to the
snare of the devil in human form.

5

Living in a Virginia country village, she did not know the practices of sin as carried on in the great centers of vice. At the age of fifteen she made a vigorous effort to get saved and longed to live a good life, but she knew nothing of the way of salvation, and every effort on the part of others was to drag her down. If it had been a horse or a mule that had fallen, they would have been given another chance, but there was no one to help her to her feet. She had never heard a real gospel sermon in her life till she came to the Rescue Home, and the first time the poor girl was told that God loved her, it broke her heart. She very soon sought and found Christ in His great Salvation.

Beloved, do you imagine that our joy is small when the Lord permits us to give these friendless girls the gospel the first time they have heard the real truth? Can you imagine the inexpressible pleasure it is to see them embrace Christ and devour the truth as fast as it can be given to them? Many of these dear girls are not only beautiful, but smart and intelligent; and after they are saved become so polished and refined in both manners and appearance that you would never think for a moment that they had ever known sin.

Hallie is of a most beautiful, modest Christian spirit. She is an example to all around her. Some time since when she was on her knees scrubbing the kitchen floor, and at the same time praying and praising God for what He had done for her, she raised up, sat back on the floor, and received her call to be a missionary. It was an appropriate place for her to receive the call, for missionaries find much scrubbing to do. May the blessed Holy Ghost qualify, and send her forth as a flaming herald of the same wonderful gospel which has so gloriously saved her. 'Reader, can she have your sympathy and prayers?

To the Lord be all the glory.

GROUP OF GIRLS AND MISSIONARIES.

FROM AN ATTIC TO A MANSION.

A SLUM missionary turned into a certain street in Chicago, then through a narrow passageway to outside stairs, which led her up to a low, studded, dingy attic, where a young widow was lying on her deathbed. Her four little children and her aged mother all slept in that one little room. She was dying with cancer, without God, and without hope. They were destitute of food, only as it was carried to them.

Since the death of her husband, two years before, she had left the little ones through the day with their old grandmother, and she had earned their meager support with her needle in a "sweat shop." The washing, ironing, and sewing for her own family of six, she would do during the night, while her babies were asleep, and when her weary body should have rested. This she kept up till she was forced to take her bed. Then with no means of support, she had "rifled" away her husband's watch to get bread, and had disposed of all that was marketable. The wolf had entered the house, and Death was just outside the door.

She had been confined to her room about a

month before the missionary found her way up
those narrow stairs. Food, flowers, kind words,
and sunshine were poured into those cheerless
rooms, and on the missionary's third visit, the
poor woman was gloriously converted to Christ.
God gave her the unmistakeable witness that her
sins were all forgiven, and her name was written
in the Book of Life. The glory of God filled the
attic, and the radiance of heaven was on the sick
woman's face. How everything was changed in
those dingy quarters! The thing she had most
dreaded was to leave her darlings in this cold,
friendless world, with no relatives who would
take interest in them; but now she calmly committed them to Jesus, and felt assured that He
would care for them. From that hour she was
unspeakably happy, and a few hours later she
passed triumphantly through the " Gates of
Pearl."

Two of our missionaries were present at that
midnight hour, when the angels climbed those
stairs, and carried her blood-washed spirit from
a stuffy little attic to a mansion in the skies. While
she was dying, the missionaries fell on their knees,
and just before she breathed her life out, her old
mother gave her heart to God, and was blessedly
saved.

That was a strange scene of mingled joy and sorrow. The little eight-year-old sat through those dark hours of the night and watched her mother die, and then got down on her knees and gave her own heart to God. That was a striking midnight scene in town. Chicago was as quiet as she ever gets, but there was a great jubilee on high.

When the children who were sleeping in the little bed were aroused and moved out into the little kitchen, the three-year-old said, " I want my mamma — I want my mamma; " then the others took it up, and such a wailing and weeping for mamma has seldom ever been witnessed. It was most pathetic, and even heart-rending. Four of the slum missionaries, all ladies, were the pall-bearers, and the funeral was most beautiful. What a transformation! What a transportation! How transcendently glorious!

But what if there had been no missionaries, or, what if they had not found her? " Pray ye the Lord of the harvest to send forth more laborers into the harvest."

Come now, and let us reason together, saith the Lord: though your sins be as scarlet, they shall be as white as snow; though they be red like crimson, they shall be as wool. Isa. 1 : 18.

FROM A SALOON TO HELL.

A BRIGHT, intelligent girl listened attentively to the gospel at one of our Sunday night street meetings in the slums. Her face indicated that she belonged to good society, but her clothes revealed that all was lost, and that she was a victim of the slums.

At the close of the service she asked one of the missionaries if she could have a private interview with her about her soul. She was told about Rest Cottage, and invited to come at once, to which she replied, " If I go, you must first go with me for my jacket."

Several of the missionaries went with her. She led them into an alley dark enough to make one's flesh crawl. They instinctively drew near to each other as they groped their way through the rayless narrow pass. Finally they reached the dismal den; a place about seven by ten feet, and not suitable for dogs to live in. The room contained a bed, chair frame, with bottom out, an old broken cook stove, and a dingy lamp on a shelf. On the bed was an old negro man, and standing in the center of the room was a white American woman, whose very appearance showed that she was once a lady, but sin had done its worst, and there was nothing left but the shadow of the past.

Maggie said to the woman, " I am tired of sin, and I am going with these missionaries," and asked her to go also, but she declined. From there she led them to another house to get her hat, as she was bareheaded. After climbing two flights of filthy stairs, they entered a room where the tobacco smoke was so dense that at first they could hardly distinguish a man from a woman. In this dismal haunt there proved to be one woman, and four men. Some of them white(?), and some of them negroes.

Here Maggie repeated what she had said in the other dive. It was not long till she was comfortably situated in Rest Cottage. There has never been a more modest, humble, reserved lovable girl in the Home than was Maggie. Her bearing and deportment was that of a lady in every respect. She was a high-school graduate, and a niece of a United States Senator, but the leprosy of sin had devoured her womanhood, and the power of appetite, passion, and habit had dragged her down to the level of negro brutes.

Think of her on commencement day, in her beautiful graduating suit, covered all over with beautiful bouquets, thrown at her by a large circle

of admiring friends and relatives! Then think
of her in the crime and squalor of a negro brothel.
" How are the ' beautiful ' fallen! "

" Once *she* was pure as the snow, but she fell,
　Fell like the snowflakes from heaven to hell ;
　Fell to be tramped like the filth of the street ;
　Fell to be scoffed, to be spit on and beat.
　Pleading, cursing, dreading to die,
　Selling her soul to whoever may buy.
　Dealing in shame for a morsel of bread,
　Hating the living, yet fearing the dead.
　Merciful God! has she fallen so low ?
　And yet she was once like the beautiful snow.

　Once *she* was fair as the beautiful snow ;
　Eyes like its crystals — a heart like its glow ;
　Once *she* was loved for her innocent grace,
　Flattered and sought for the charm of her face.
　Father, mother, sisters and all,
　God and herself she has lost by her fall.
　Wickedest wretch that goes shivering by,
　Takes a wide sweep lest she wander too nigh ;
　All of her vileness we read and we know,
　There's naught that is pure but the beautiful snow."

She came to the Home expressly for salvation,
and made a determined, desperate fight to conquer
her appetite for strong drink, but the smoldering
fires of rum would break out again and again,

and perhaps while preparing a meal, she would suddenly rush to the matron and say, " Oh, I want to go out and get a drink. I am burning up inside."

On one of these occasions they fell on their knees, and although the very atmosphere seemed charged with the power of hell, they cried to God for deliverance till the answer came. When Maggie attempted to pray, it was more like the screech of an animal than a human voice. Convulsed with the raging appetite for drink, she fought her way through a regiment of devils, and touched God for deliverance.

For a time she seemed to walk in great victory, but later, circumstances arose which divulged her association with a negro man. The humiliation seemed too great, and she broke away, and took to drink.

This was the chance of her life to confess all and get right with God, but she stifled her convictions, and forever lost her opportunity. Sins confessed, are forgiven and forgotten; but sins covered, never die, but will dog your steps till the day of your death, take you by the throat when you are dying, and lock you up in hell when you are dead. Poor Maggie had her last chance.

It was not long till her brains were dashed out by a negro man in a saloon. Her brains were shoveled up off that floor like so much sawdust; her body sent to the morgue, and a nameless grave in the potter's field, and her soul to hell.

A BUMMY BUM.

A BUMMY BUM.

THE subject of this sketch challenges all skepticism and unbelief as to the power of the gospel to renew and reconstruct the most wrecked and ruined life and furnishes a marvelous example of how broken and scattered homes may be made whole, and blasted hopes may be restored.

Reared among the hills of southern Ohio in a religious home where there was no salvation, he formed a strong disrelish for a mere form or empty profession of religion. He was often under direst conviction for sin, but there was no one to tell him the way of real salvation. His childish heart often longed for deliverance. He wept and sobbed many a lone hour, but no one ever told him how to get rid of sin.

At the age of thirteen he left home and started out to see this great lost world. He had no difficulty in finding it, but it was all so cold his young heart hardened and his feet took hold of the ways of death. When a young man starts down, he finds many to push him lower, but very few are ready to help him on his feet again. He sank lower and lower in sin until life was a great burden. Many times he stood on the border of eternity with nothing in the world to hold him back from suicide but the fear of hell.

After years of wandering and dissipation in drunkenness and revelry, God made a vigorous attempt to turn him back from this awful life by the death of his father. Over the casket he promised God with tears that he would turn and be a better man, but before the day was ended he was trying to drink consolation from a jug of whisky. It was impossible for him to keep his vows, he was bound with fetters of strong drink until there was no earthly power that could free him.

A second time God warned him by the death of his precious little boy. He says, "As the frozen clods covered the baby casket from my view once more God's Spirit pleaded with me and again I said, ' I will be a better man.' But the chains of sin bound me and there was no power that could break them, it was impossible. Within fourteen hours after the funeral, I was drinking as before. A few weeks later my wife, disgusted and discouraged, took our little girl, then three and one-half years old, and went back to her mother. Without her knowledge I loaded all our household goods in a box car, shipped them to another state, sold them at auction for fifteen dollars and went and got drunk. I have never seen my loved ones since; it has been almost five years, and in my sober moments my heart has often longed for the fellowship of my wife and baby. I wandered on as a man lost in a trackless desert, until I became a common tramp and brought up in the slimiest slums of Chicago among the bummiest dens of sin, without home, without wife, friends or loved ones and only clothes enough to answer for an excuse, hatless and shoeless, without a garment fit to put on a cur dog, shivering with the winter cold, I was ready for the morgue and the suicide's grave in the potter's field."

After being absent from church for years, he sought relief by attending church services, but all in vain. He went into a Presbyterian church, hoping to find food for his soul, but the preacher preached that night on "McKinley," and his poor starving soul found no food. If the minister had preached " Jesus " instead of " McKinley," the young man would doubtless have been saved. He went into church after church hoping to find help, but nothing was offered but husks. He finally went into the Trinity Methodist church of Cincinnati, oh, so hungry, thinking certainly he would get soul food here, but to his dismay the learned doctor lectures on his " trip through Europe," and

6

the young tramp turned away from all churches in despair. How little the preachers of these times know who is listening when they are lecturing, instead of preaching the gospel! In a recent conversation he said, " I never saw one who was really saved until I was more than twenty years old, not one, preachers not excepted."

He loved his wife and children tenderly, but the demon drink caused him to neglect and desert them. His wife was true to him and remained with him as long as there was hope of bread and water. At one time he braced up long enough to save one hundred and eighty-seven dollars, intending to send for his wife and children, hoping to have a home again, but came to Chicago and in two weeks it was all gone. Each time he went lower and lower in sin. One time he put on good clothes and secured employment in a certain large firm, but stole a large sum of money and fled to another city.

Tired of tramping, he once took employment at a freight house on the dock where ships were unloaded in Chicago. It was night work and late in the autumn and sometimes not much to do. He said: " My conviction for sin was so great that many a time I have rolled on the dirty cement floor of that old freight house and wept and cried for mercy by the hour, but I did not know how to find relief."

One night he was wandering down State Street when he heard one of our preachers preaching the gospel and a sister sang " There is wonderful power in the Blood." He listened enough to hear that there was hope and as the man closed his remarks he announced that there were Apostolic noon meetings held every day at the corner of Clark and Washington Streets at noon. For several days he went around and stood at the foot of the stairs, but afraid to go inside where the services were being held. Finally he ventured in, took a back seat, and for the first time in his life heard the full gospel. His heart was somewhat tendered, but he was powerless to move. He said, " If the papers had been made out, signed, sealed, and delivered for me to go to hell, I could not have gone forward." The meeting closed and he turned away in despair.

For weeks he wandered through the streets, homeless and friendless. It was coming on winter, his feet were on the ground, his clothes were not sufficient to protect him from freezing. He again thought to commit suicide, but something restrained him.

Standing on the Van Buren Street bridge about

four o'clock on the morning of December 20th, his eyes were attracted to a card lying at his feet. He picked it up and scraped off enough of the frozen mud to enable him to read: "The wages of sin is death, but the gift of God is eternal life through Jesus Christ our Lord." He turned it over and read: "Come unto me all ye that labor and are heavy laden and I will give you rest. 499 State Street, Apostolic Mission." He stood there in the cold and wept like a broken-hearted child. Sin had blasted his life. The world had nothing to offer him. He attempted to cry to God, but could receive no answer. When he attempted to pray, Satan said: "It is too late, you have crossed the dead line, here you are a drunken bum with no place to lay your head, no one will ever take you in." But again something repeated the words of the card: "I will give you rest."

How little our missionary thought when she dropped the card the day before who would read it! That night he went to the mission and three nights later found himself at the penitent form where God gloriously saved him. It was Christmas eve and the most wonderful Christmas eve he had ever seen. For years he had not passed a Christmas without drunkenness, but here he found the gift of God, the Saviour of the world. Hear his testimony: " He who saved the dying thief has saved me. I was a living thief, at the age of twenty-eight a drunkard, a gambler, a thief, a tramp and at last a common bum, and He has saved me from all my sins."

He very soon found employment in the yards of the Rock Island Railroad Company. After a few weeks they asked him to work on Sunday, but by this time he was seeking the experience of entire sanctification and said: " No, I can not work on Sunday." The result was he was thrown out of employment. He soon obtained work in a cooper shop, but after a few days they put him to make wine-casks and he said: " I have been emptying wine-casks for years and I can not aid in making them," and again he was out of a job.

In the meantime, he received the baptism of the Holy Ghost and was sanctified wholly. From that hour God put the message of full salvation upon his lips and he went to preaching the gospel that had so wonderfully saved him from a life of sin. He said: " Brother Rees, I am going to North Dakota where I can get work on the farm and earn honest money and keep the Sabbath." In two or three weeks I received a letter from the trustees of the University buildings of the University of North Dakota, stating that a certain Chase Hall had applied for the position of janitorship and had given me as reference. Many would have thought it impossible to recommend such a drunken scoundrel, but I told them the truth and said that I considered him perfectly trusty as long as he remained as well saved as when he left us. The next thing I heard was that he had the position and was preaching on the street from three to five times a week. God has marvelously blessed him as a street preacher of the gospel of Jesus Christ.

This is a sample of what God is doing in the slums. He is taking both men and women from saloons, dance halls and brothels, saving, sanctifying, and healing them, and sending them back into those same districts to preach this gospel which is the power of God in the slums.

To Father, Son, and Holy Ghost be all the glory forever.

LULU.

LULU — A STRANGE STORY.

LULU —— was born and brought up in New York City. Her mother died when she was four years old. Her father was a pronounced infidel, and she was thoroughly schooled in this unreasonable heresy. She had no knowledge of the truth and had never heard the real gospel of Jesus Christ until she came to the Rescue Home.

She was an unusually bright child. She finished grammar school at the age of fifteen and went out to work, first as a nurse girl, then as a housekeeper. She was welcomed back home only when she could turn in a good sum of money from her earnings. This she grew tired of and obtained a position as a traveling agent for a humane society. It was in one of the public parks of Chicago that she met a man who with flattering words and fair speeches led her into sin under promise of marriage. Then to shield himself and the name of his family, he insisted that she must put the baby away for a year or two, and after they had been married for a time they would adopt the child as from an orphanage. She loved the child and said she would not desert it under any circumstances. Her mother instinct, true to womanhood, would rather have the child and suffer the shame than to have the man who would desert his own.

While she was in the city hospital, a girl in the same ward received a letter from the Rescue Home. She told her about the place and the kindness of the good ladies there and Lulu determined to find the place if possible. Infidel that she was, she was saved within two days after she entered the home. She went on fine for a time and could hardly see the need of a second work of grace. She was having such a royal good time with her first experience that a second to her would seem almost superfluous.

But one day, under provocation, she grew angry and was at once convicted for sanctification. This conviction deepened until it was most distressing. Finally her soul hunger increased and the blackness of darkness became so unbearable she said "something must be done." She was cook that day and was making pumpkin pies. They were all filled and ready for the oven, when she could endure it no longer. She said she was sick, called for another cook, went upstairs, threw herself on the floor and never arose until she was sanctified wholly.

As soon as the fire fell upon her soul, she ran downstairs and sat down on the floor and told the matron all about it. It was most thrilling. Already the Spirit had been talking to her about change in her dress and manner of life. She had a worldly dress that cost her thirty-five dollars. One day she had worn it to the service. She said she saw the preacher look at it and she interpreted his look to mean she must never wear that dress to the service again.

She has changed in all her manner of life and has become conformed to the will and image of the Lord, until she is a marvelous exhibition of divine grace. She writes and reads German as well as English, but best of all, she knows the language of Canaan, and testifies that she is saved and sanctified wholly. We will never cease to praise the Lord for her beautiful life.

To Father, Son, and Holy Ghost be all the glory.

MARGARET ROLLER.

MARGARET ROLLER, OR FROM THE GUTTER TO HOLINESS.

MARGARET ROLLER was born in Ireland. Her ancestors were Catholics for several generations. She came to America at twenty years of age, a fine specimen of Irish womanhood. She married, and became a mother of six children, but the moderate use of strong drink created an uncontrollable appetite, and she soon became a confirmed drunkard. She sank from bad to worse until finally her husband refused to live with her. Her home was wrecked, and her children scattered, the youngest only a baby, and all under fifteen years of age. Worse than orphans, the poor little motherless things were homeless and friendless.

Margaret, a poor drunken Catholic, staggered through the streets and crept through the allies in the cold and wet of the darkest night. Reeling down Chestnut Street, not knowing where, and caring less, no hope of anything better, it was an awful night of blackness and darkness when she staggered near the church, and a good brother invited her to come inside.

She spurned the invitation at first,— she was too good a Catholic, drunk as she was, to enter a

Protestant church, but she was wet and cold, and the brother was so kind and persistent that she finally yielded, and was helped to a seat in the church. When the service was adjourned, she had no place to go, and was too stupid to care. Two of the brethren offered to take her to Rest Cottage, which they assured her was a beautiful home where she would be welcomed.

It was almost midnight when they succeeded in getting her to the Home. The matron and missionaries had retired, but were soon at their post to give her a warm welcome, a hot bath, and put her in a clean bed. Poor Margaret was not able to appreciate anything that night, but when she awoke amid the new surroundings, it was almost like heaven to her. The kindness and attention of the missionaries touched her deeply, and made lasting impressions upon her mind. Day by day she loosened her grip upon her religious faith, and little by little her eyes were opened to the awful delusion of the training of her life. On the ninth day she was gloriously converted and gave up her Catholicism entirely.

All appetite for drink was at once taken from her, and she became an entirely new woman. Her husband was a drinking man, but was not such a

sot as she was. He had refused to recognize her
on the streets, or answer her letters. He would
tear them up without even reading them.

It was not long after she was saved till she was
sanctified wholly. One day she felt led to write
her husband once more, and make a full confession of all the wrongs of her life. When he
received the letter, instead of tearing it up as usual,
he felt strangely impressed to read it. Its contents
touched his heart deeply, and he somehow felt
that possibly there was hope for poor Margaret
after all. He was finally induced to meet her at
the home of Brother D——, where a beautiful
wedding dinner was served. The result was the
salvation of her husband and the reunion of the
family.

A house was soon furnished, and the six scattered little tots were gathered together in the cosy
little home where all are so happy to-day. It was
my privilege recently, to shout and pray in their
home, and the five little ones present all knelt in
a row, as devout as saints.

During their worst dissipation, they lived in
Pawtucket, but when they were happily settled in
their little home in Providence, the little three-
year-old, who was so thoroughly enjoying the new

7

situation, said to Margaret one day, " Mamma, isn't it too bad that God is not in Pawtucket? " It is the power of Christ in the slums. Let everything that hath breath give glory to God.

THANKSGIVING DINNER IN THE SLUMS.

THANKSGIVING IN CHICAGO SLUMS.

THIS was one of the greatest days of my life. After our missionaries had sent out well-filled baskets of food to twenty-seven families of the worthy poor, we all loaded ourselves down with roasted turkey and all the " fixings " that go with a turkey dinner and started to the Harrison Street Police Station. We had sent some of the workers and provisions on ahead to be cooked in the jail, but we were still loaded until we attracted the attention of the public on the streets and in the cars. For once we were a gazing stock, but joy so flooded our souls that it had no effect on us.

The officials of the prison were very kind and in a short time the table was loaded with a steaming dinner. The chief matron of the Chicago force was there to greet and assist us. It was a sight I will never forget. One poor girl not more than fifteen years old said she had dreamed of turkey the night before, but, of course, had no hope of seeing one. Some of the girls wept and sobbed so they could hardly eat. Poor girls, the memory of other thanksgivings rushed in upon them and broke their hearts.

When they were all at the table, we had prayer

and while one of the missionaries played the organ and sang "The day will soon be over, the digging will be done," the police matron, a noble-hearted woman wept with us over this touching scene. Several gave their hearts to God during the day.

We overheard some of the men who were fed in their cells, talking about the great kindness of those who had remembered them, and they were deeply touched. We have rescued five girls within one week, and four of them are beautifully saved. I tell this to the glory of God and to the comfort of those all over the land who are giving to the support of this work.

To Father, Son, and Holy Ghost be all the glory forever.

RESCUED FROM CHICAGO JAIL.

RESCUED FROM CHICAGO JAIL.

MANY who will read these lines have been deeply interested in the poor, starving family which was rescued from the witness cell in the Harrison Street Police Station. The cut accompanying this sketch is from a picture made after their condition was somewhat improved, but still showing the lines of starvation.

When we determined to take them, and trust God for the means of support, the police authorities said " That is real charity," and proposed to send them to the depot, and then telephoned to the Austin patrol to meet the train at Austin Station and convey them to the home we had provided for their care.

Of course, one of our missionaries must accompany them to see them safely through their journey. When they were lifted into the patrol, the missionary climbed in with them and the police exclaimed with astonishment: " You are not going to ride in the patrol, are you? " " Certainly," she said, " why not? " That is what full salvation does. Followed by a curious throng through the streets, she was made a spectacle to angels and men.

The baby sitting in its mother's lap was too far gone. After two weeks it went to be with Jesus. The remainder of the family recovered and after a few weeks we set them up to housekeeping in a small way. How grateful they seemed for all the kindness shown them! There is a joy that comes from helping others that is never known by those who think only of themselves.

"He that giveth to the poor lendeth to the Lord." What an investment it must be to place funds with Him. He will certainly see that the returns are ample.

CHRISTINE.

CHRISTINE, A BROKEN-HEARTED GIRL.

CHRISTINE —— was born of Christian parents in the State of Wisconsin. Her mother died when she was twelve years old. It was not very long until a step-mother made it very unpleasant for the poor girl in the home. She determined that the only way to keep peace in the family was for her to leave home. She found employment as a saleslady, first in Milwaukee and then in Chicago.

Brought up in the church, she was a great worker in the Epworth League, on the Social Committee, regular at all church services, faithful in all the church entertainments, was a member of the popular quartet and most diligent in her efforts to increase the attendance of the church services.

Finally the influence of the church socials gave her a liking for more worldly entertainments and she soon found herself in circles of worldliness and sin. Now and then she found it convenient to take a glass of wine. On Thanksgiving eve she was in attendance at a party where she thought her womanhood and virtue were in perfect safety.

But late in the evening a drug was slipped into her glass of wine and she was soon unconscious.

When she awoke the next day, it was only to disappointment and sorrow, for she found herself forever hopelessly ruined. There is no language to express the feelings of this poor heart-broken girl as the real situation dawned upon her. She had gradually step by step deviated from her early training and she now found herself helpless and hopeless in the embrace of ruin.

Filled with unutterable sorrow and with not a ray of hope for anything worth living for, she turned upon the guilty party and with words almost too strong for us to repeat told him that there was not a place in hell hot enough for him. She says, " If I had been capable of murder, I would have killed him on the spot."

Her next impression was to commit suicide, but God mercifully withheld her from this awful deed. The world was a wilderness of blackness and darkness, and about that time her father, her only earthy friend was taken home to heaven.

Homeless, friendless and sick, she was thrown into the Cook County Hospital. It was here a kind lady told her of Rest Cottage and of Jesus who was able to save. She was brought to the

Rescue Home in Chicago, but seemed slow to yield to the convictions of the Spirit.

She was listening to a sermon on the fifty-third chapter of Isaiah, when suddenly she seemed to see Jesus dying on the cross for her. All she would have to surrender loomed up before her. All she seemed to have in the world was her darling baby, which she loved tenderly. When she saw that she must give her all, including the baby, to Jesus she hesitated; it seemed the hardest thing of her life to give up her only comfort. But late at night, she was induced to say, "Yes, my baby and all, I yield to God forever." The peace and happiness that came streaming into her soul was something beyond all expression. When she retired, the baby was in usual health and her soul was flooded with the sunlight of glory. When she awoke the next morning, her darling baby was dead on her arm, but the glory of God was still in her soul and she said, "What I did last night in giving my baby to the Lord stands forever."

That was a most touching funeral. She had no thought when she said yes to God that He would so soon take her darling, but her soul never drew back. From that day, she made rapid advance in divine grace. She soon received a distinct call to God's work, and the burning, passionate love for fallen girls has so consumed her whole being that it seems at times that she will die if she is not able to save the lost.

It was made so plain to us that the hand of the Lord was upon her in preparation for soul winning that we have sent her to the Bible School to be trained for this work of rescuing the perishing.

In the school she proved herself worthy of her calling, and she will soon go forth to the great harvest field to labor for souls.

Praise the Lord.

A SLUM FEAST — CHICAGO BUMS EATING CHRISTMAS DINNER.

"A SLUM FEAST."

A FEW years ago my attention was called to Luke 14: 13, where Jesus was teaching the divine principles of New Testament salvation. Here I made the startling discovery that very few of us are practically "Bible Christians." Many years ago I had covenanted to be a Bible Christian, and to walk in all the light received. This seemed to me like a new revelation. "When thou makest a dinner or a supper, call not thy friends, nor thy brethren, neither thy kinsmen, nor thy rich neighbors; lest they also bid thee again. But when thou makest a feast, call the poor, the maimed, the lame, the blind; and thou shalt be blessed; for they can not recompense thee; for thou shalt be recompensed at the resurrection of the just."

Here I was convicted to practice, literally, the contents of this Scripture. Christmas was approaching. Chicago was spending fourteen million dollars for gifts alone, and everybody who could were making preparations for Christmas turkey dinners. I said to my family, we will not have turkey this Christmas, we will defer our dinner and spend Christmas in the slums. We announced that at twelve o'clock on Christmas

Day the Mission in the slums on lower State Street would be opened, and a free dinner would be furnished to all homeless men.

Long before twelve o'clock, the street was thronged. The bums, thugs, tramps, and red-nosed drunkards of every description, in tattered garments, rags, and vermin, waited in zero weather for the door to open. Many of them were college bred. Doctors, lawyers, merchants, mechanics, and some from the best of homes, and in fact they were there from almost every walk of life. When the door was opened, with uncovered heads they marched in as orderly as a congregation of Quakers or Presbyterians. When the Mission was filled to the utmost capacity, the doors were closed. When all were seated at the long, well-filled tables, they politely bowed their heads while we asked God's blessing upon the food.

While a dozen of our mission workers served them with hot coffee and a palatable dinner, we preached to them the gospel of Christ. Many were the touching and pathetic scenes as their eyes filled with tears on account of the kindness shown them by the Christian workers.

When all were satisfied, we were forced to turn them out in the cold, and filled the Mission a

second time with those who had stood out in the
wintry blast. This was done a third, fourth, and
fifth time. Each Mission full were prayed with,
and preached to, and satisfied with the good things
of the table.

Strong men as well as boys were seen choking
with vivid recollections of their mothers and
sisters, as our young women so freely served them.
Many eyes were wet with tears at the remem-
brance of other Christmas days, their well-filled
stockings in the "old chimney corner," and the
sweet voices ringing out, "I wish you a Merry
Christmas."

Most people say it is folly to feed such worthless
wretches, but as a result of that one dinner, seven
of those men were brought to God that day. That
dinner proved a wonderful quickening to the
spiritual life of the Mission, and a wonderful
incentive to activity in service.

That dinner cost about thirty-five dollars out
side of some donations of food. That was five
dollars a head for the souls that were saved that
day. You may say that a "Bum" is not worth
five dollars, but if he should be standing inside the
"Gates of Pearl" to greet us when we arrive in
heaven, we will think then that he is worth it. It
was the kindness that broke their hearts. They

were accustomed to everything else. You could not phase them with a policeman's club, or subdue them with a seven shooter, but kind words and deeds melted and conquered the most hardened hearts.

One of the men who was converted that day was an atheist, said he never had believed in God or religion, but when he saw the kindness shown to fallen men that day, he said there must be something in it, and sought and found God.

Beloved, those fellows do not need to be told about the "fall of man," "original sin," or an "endless hell," they have acres of hell in their own hearts. They need some one to love them, and tell them there is hope. Beloved, are you a Christian? Are you not a member of some orthodox church? Then who is invited when there is a feast in your home? Who is it that eats turkey with you at Thanksgiving and at Christmas time? Who is present at your birthday dinners and wedding anniversaries? Is it your children, and their children? Or your neighbors, who are as able to make a feast as yourselves?

When did the poor, the lame, and the outcasts of earth feast with you?

THREE SLUM MISSIONARIES.

LILLIE, A FRIENDLESS GIRL.

SOME of the most clinging, dependent characters are found among the fallen girls of this land.
Their very lovely, loving, clinging dispositions
have been the avenue through which Satan has
performed his subtle, fiendish work. Many a girl
is so artless and innocent that she is led into sin
almost before she is aware of it. One of the
noblest characteristics of womanhood is the
strength of her affectionate nature. The affections
of a young girl, between the ages of thirteen and
eighteen are easily won by kindness and flattery
and a man who will trifle with a woman's affections is destitute of true manhood, and has little
more soul than a brute. But "wicked men and
seducers are waxing worse and worse," and hundreds of beastly men play with a woman's affections as if they were of small consequence.

It was one of these heartless demons in human
form that led our dear Lillie to the slaughter.
How much kinder it would have been for him to
have shot her head off with a gun. Her mother
died when she was four years old; her father was
a gambling, drinking man, and gambled away two
or three good homes. Her stepmother disliked

her because she looked like her mother. She endured the unpleasantness at home and remained in school until at the age of seventeen her father refused to clothe her and in an awful fit of anger swore that he would do nothing more for her. She was forced out in the cold world to make her own way.

She obtained employment, first at seventy-five cents per week, and out of her small earnings managed to send some money home each week, which her father gambled and drank up. When her little half-sister died, there was no money to bury her and Lillie buried the child and worked out the price of the funeral outfit by the week.

The villain who ruined her was the mayor's son. He met her first in the round dance. It was to her the dance of death. It has proven thus to thousands of American daughters. What a hot-bed of lust is the parlor dance, indulged in by so many so-called Christians (?). The fruits of dancing, and the experience of tens of thousands prove that men do not have women in their arms in the round dance without having impure feelings. Many a mother has planned the dancing-party in her own parlor that has started her children into a life of impurity. Many a man will dance with hundreds of women, but when he comes to marry, he does not want a dancing wife. Why? Because he does not want a wife who has been in the arms of all of the men of the neighborhood. It is time the girls of America were demanding the same standard of purity in their husbands, as is demanded of them. Sister, why should you consent to marry a man who has hugged and waltzed with all the dancing-women in town?

Many a time Lillie longed to be a Christian, but she came in contact with so much sham religion, and never met the genuine, that she knew not the way of salvation. She worked in the home of a minister who not only drank beer and was mean in his family, but made such advances toward her as to make her know that he was a bad man.

When ruined and deserted by those who should have protected her, she attempted suicide by turning on the gas, but was rescued just in time to save her life. She lived in a Hoosier city, but when the mayor and his son had turned her down, everybody who knew her turned from her. Not an earthly friend did she have who stood by her. The mayor seemed especially averse to this friendless girl whom his son had ruined. Everybody

took the side of the young villain, as is commonly
the case. The poor, heart-broken child started
out, she hardly knew where.

When she arrived in Chicago, she walked the
streets a perfect stranger, among two million people; she wept and wrung her hands and sobbed
aloud. She walked block after block; some would
stop and look, but it was only a woman in trouble,
and nobody had time even to ask a question. She
saw a policeman, and thought she would tell him
her story, and ask his advice, but he was such a
vicious-looking officer that the poor girl was
afraid of him. She walked on, and wept and
wrung her hands, and tried to pray, but she
knew not the way of salvation. She saw another
officer, and he was not quite so cross-looking, and
weeping as if her heart would break, she told him
her story, and begged him to do something for
her. He pressed a button and called the patrol,
and she was thrown into the famous Harrison
Street Police Station, and there she lay in that
dingy jail from Sunday till Wednesday.

The matron of the station is a noble-hearted
woman, and is a warm friend of our rescue work.
She sent word to our missionaries, and one of them
went to the station, and Lillie says from the mo-

ment she looked upon her face, she saw she had something she had never seen in any one's face before. When asked if she would come to Rest Cottage, she said, "Certainly; I have no other place to go." That very night she stood up in a public meeting, and with streaming eyes requested prayer. It was not long until she was wonderfully saved. She has since been sanctified wholly, clearly called, and is a divinely qualified mission worker.

We placed her in the Bible School until she felt she must go into the slums to preach Jesus to the fallen. She is now a regular ordained deaconness of the International Apostolic Holiness Union, and has been a most successful missionary in the slums. For some months she has traveled as an evangelist, and God has marvelously blessed her labors in the salvation of souls. Whole families have turned to God, erected a family altar, and have thrown wide open their hearts and doors and offered Lillie a home. Whether she stands in the pulpit facing five hundred people, or in the court room facing a stern-looking judge and a jury of twelve men, she always brings the house down, when with streaming eyes she tells them her own story. It is enough to melt a heart of stone.

The following are a few incidents of her experience in the slums: —

"I visited a mother and children in poverty. She had kept her children from starvation by securing the crumbs from the tables of a restaurant. The little baby had had no milk for two days; its hands and face were pinched with hunger. I gave them a little relief, and prayed with them." How much can be accomplished with a very little means in the slums. A hod of coal, a three-cent loaf of bread, or a pint of milk for the baby, may bring tears of gratitude to their eyes, and tide them over a crisis.

.   .   .   .

"I found a poor sick woman and little children entirely destitute. I handed her some money, and began talking to her about the salvation of her soul. She laid the money on the table, and her hungry soul listened to every word. She soon fell upon her knees and wept her way to Calvary. God wonderfully saved her soul. When she arose from her knees, I called her attention to the fact that the children were playing with the money. She said, 'I had forgotten all about it. I needed the money, but I needed salvation so much more, and I've got it now.' Glory to God.

.   .   .   .

"I felt led to go to a certain house of shame, but was refused admittance. I went several times, but was never permitted to enter. One day while working in another part of the city, I suddenly felt led to turn and go to that house again. When I stood at the door the madam said to the girl who opened it, 'Yes, tell them they are welcome to-day.' Satan instantly suggested that they wanted me for a purpose, and that I would never get out, but the courage of God rose up in my soul, and I fearlessly walked in. When I told them my experience,— what a discouraged, wrecked life I had lived, and that Jesus had saved me, all five of them broke down and wept under the power of God. We are welcome in that house."

It is the power of the gospel in the slums.

MISS M——.

MISS M——.

PREACHING to the female prisoners in the Chicago jail, I observed a girl about nineteen years of age, with an unusual face and symmetrical form, elegantly dressed in silk, for whom I was especially drawn out in prayer. Her manner and bearing were in striking contrast with all the surroundings. Everything indicated that she was from the better walks of life. At first she was defiant, and showed signs of an attempt to lead the prisoners in a bit of sport. I silently breathed one short prayer, " Blessed Holy Ghost, save that girl, and make her a missionary." Within a few minutes she was on her knees, and in tears crying out to God for mercy.

After a little conversation with her, I went to the chief matron and said, " What can I do for M——? " She answered, " There is nothing you can do. Her crime is grand larceny, and she must go to the State's prison." I said, " It is too bad; I wish I could do something for her." She insisted there was nothing I could do.

When I returned the following Sabbath, to my surprise M—— was still there. According to the usual custom she should have been removed to the county jail. The captain said it was a mistake. I saw in it a divine providence. After another opportunity of prayer and conversation with the poor heart-broken girl, I felt sure that she had had her lesson, and that Christ could and would save her. The second time I went to the matron, and said, " I want to do something for M——; " but, as before, she said, " There is nothing you can do."

I went to the captain; he seemed like a gentleman, but said he was powerless. He sent me to the detective who had made the arrest. He received me kindly, but sent me to the chief of the Bureau of Detectives, who was not very approachable, and seemed to me quite heartless in his attitude toward the girls. He said, " Such girls are no good; you had just as well let her go to the penitentiary." But I begged that she might have another chance. He finally sent me to the Judge of the court, and he referred me to another judge. I thought I saw that it was to get rid of me, but did not feel at liberty to give up the chase.

I went home tired out, and tried to think that I had done my duty, but the next morning I found myself on the path to secure that girl. The second judge had referred me to the clerk of the court, and he had no more to do with it than I had, but he assured me the state's attorney was the man I wanted to see. The state's attorney sent me to the grand jury, and the grand jury refused to see me. I finally saw that if I obtained her at all, it must be under suspended sentence, so I asked that her case be brought into court; but the only promise that I could secure was, that I would be notified when her case was to come up.

Just then I was compelled to go to Boston to hold a convention. I charged my head missionary to appear in the court, and plead for M—— as she would for an own sister. The missionary at that time was not as familiar with judges and juries as she is to-day. When the notice was received, she went into her closet and prayed, and went into court and preached Jesus until they were glad to give her the girl, to get rid of her. You may imagine that my heart leaped with joy when the message reached me that M—— was safe in the Home.

She soon began writing letters of apology, making wrongs right by returning stolen articles, until finally God wonderfully saved her soul. Poor girl! How she suffered with remorse. She soon felt called to missionary work, and we sent her to the Bible Training School instead of to the penitentiary. Do you not think that was far better? In the Bible School she conducted herself in a very commendable manner, and made good progress in her studies. But the power of habit was so strong that she made one break and went down. But God put her on her feet again. Soon after leaving the Bible School she was taken ill, and for sixteen long weeks lay in the hospital a great sufferer. But here God talked to her about His will for her in the future, and she was led into a depth and solidity of Christian experience which she had not known.

When she recovered her strength sufficiently, the Lord opened the way for her to take a position as assistant matron of a Rescue Home for girls. How God does honor those who honor Him, regardless of what they have been.

After a time she was sent to a Deaconess' Training School in Washington, D. C., for further preparation for the work. When she was through her course of study, she went into the slums of New York City, where she is a faithful missionary of the Cross to-day. Her spirit is covered with the radiance of heaven, and her face is glowing with the splendors of divine grace. To Father, Son and Holy Ghost be all the glory forever.

REST COTTAGE, 123 HOWARD AVENUE, CHICAGO.

BERNIE.

THE subject of this sketch baffles all human imagination, and all power of description. Her unselfish nature would, out of respect for her relatives whom she feels she has greatly injured, withhold her name from the reading public. She submits to publication this strange story of her life only to glorify God, and magnify the grace of His Son, who has saved her from all sin, and whom she worships and adores above all others. Beloved, it gives me great pleasure to testify that this daughter of sorrow is unwavering in her devotion, loyalty, and fidelity to Christ.

Born of a typical aristocratic southern family, at one time a daughter of wealth, she was naturally very proud, but kind and affectionate. After her father's death, through some designing agent, the wealth was swept away, and she was left to the mercy of her two half-brothers. She was greatly loved and favored by all the older members of the family, and her widowed mother gave her a most guarded training. She did not want for proper discipline, and her devoted mother gave her all the religious light she herself had. Bernie says, " I attach no blame to my mother's training, but like many other poor girls, his Satanic Majesty got too strong hold on me, and like a dew-drop I fell from heaven to hell."

Her fall was not because of weakness of character or volition, as is often the case. She had an iron will, and when pursuing her chosen subject, it seemed impossible to turn her from it. Her passionate love for books and music, and her fixed determination to spend her life in teaching was always apparent. She entered school at the age of four, and completed a teachers' course at sixteen, with the one all-absorbing ambition to teach.

Her soul's interest was nothing to her, and she had little use for the Bible or Christianity. At one time she read the Bible and with her reasoning turn of mind thought she gave it a fair test and proved to her satisfaction that it would not stand the test of reason; and she became an infidel. But this gave her no satisfaction; there was always an inexpressible longing for something she did not find.

She taught five years in her home school, going from the primary to the principalship, successful beyond her most sanguine expectations. She had several good offers of marriage, but she refused all. It was not long till her health failed. Many of the best physicians were consulted. They all told her that her only hope of health was married life. This her whole being revolted from. She cared only to succeed in her chosen profession.

Her life was blameless, and her reputation untarnished. She lived above suspicion. Dancing was the only worldly amusement she was particularly fond of, and that was regarded in her community as perfectly innocent, but has proved the broadest and one of the most alluring and glittering roads to hell.

A rapid decline of health caused her many bitter hours, and finally she was held back from her work temporarily. Being a confirmed infidel as to a future existence, she decided to commit suicide. No act of her life was more calmly and deliberately planned than was this atrocious crime. She determined to give her brother, who was a student, a minute description of all the effects and sensations caused by taking poison. The drug was purchased and set on the table in her room. She seated herself at the table with pencil and tablet, and addressed a letter to her brother, telling him what she was about to do, and that she would describe all the symptoms and sensations as they came while consciousness lasted. She coolly and collectedly swallowed the drug, and began to write. She described symptom after symptom, until finally she said, "My sight is growing dim; I can no longer see the lines," and with a few irregular strokes, showing a vigorous attempt to continue, she dropped the pencil, and soon became unconscious. After lying in an unconscious state about two hours, she partially returned to consciousness, and then lapsed back to insensibility, in which state she remained till 7 A. M., at which time she was found in her room with a death-like look, and jaws set.

The family physician was called, restoratives used, and consciousness returned. It was greatly to her disappointment and dismay. It is very clear that it was only God who held her back from death. Unbelievable as it is, she then resolved to become some man's wife, in all but name, and if there was any truth in the physicians, she would cover her tracks, and continue her life-work as a teacher.

She soon accepted a call to teach in the northern part of the State, and it was there she met her doom. Here she met one of the leading men of the place. His Christianity was never questioned; he was trusted, loved, and revered by all who knew him. She little thought that the plans matured in her heart, and of which only God knew, would be carried out only too well here, and against her will. It was while boarding in his home she was brought under his strange, satanic, mesmeric power, and led to ruin as a lamb to slaughter.

When her ruin was accomplished and she awoke to the situation, she was plunged into the blackness and darkness of an awful horror. The dreadful anguish she suffered seemed unbearable. It would seem that it took this dreadful misfortune to wake her to the fact that she had a soul, and to the awfulness of sin. But O, how the poor girl suffered now! When she knew she must be a mother, without home, friends, a name, or qualification for such a responsibility, her grief became terrific. For the first time she felt she must have a God. If there was a God anywhere, she must have His assistance.

She began searching the Scriptures. One morning she stood and looked at the Book vaguely for a long time, and wondered if after all it were true. She picked it up, began to read, and for nearly three hours it held her spellbound. She was perfectly fascinated; the more she read, the more she believed, and God was slowly but surely melting her proud stubborn heart.

A holy woman placed in her hand a copy of a full salvation paper, and in this way she heard for the first time in her life of Rescue Work. She was entirely ignorant of the common vice in our great cities, and was greatly puzzled to know what could induce people who had never been down to devote their lives to the rescue of such unfortunate creatures. The poor girl asked what was done with the inmates, and how the Homes were supported. To her utter astonishment the lady answered, " The Lord takes care of them." This almost staggered her. She said no more, but felt deep in her soul that it was so. The good lady told her how the Lord could sanctify a human soul and keep it from sin. Again she was shocked, but said nothing, and kept on reading the Bible. The great yearning hunger to know God grew intense.

The time came for her to go to the hospital, and the loneliness of those dismal days seemed unbearable. She cried out, " O God, you must do something for me." While spending a night with a friend, overwhelmed with indescribable waves of desolation, she cried, " O God, if there is a God, you must reveal yourself to me to-night." A little real faith began to spring up in her heart as she continued in prayer, until suddenly, a burden as the weight of the world, rolled off her soul, and the glory and presence of God covered her, until the room, that was without natural light.

was really lighted with the radiance of His presence. She says: —

"I had not slept for months, but when I finished
my prayer, I fell asleep, and for twelve hours
rested like a child. I returned to my brother's
home, and determined to go to Chicago; I did
not know how I could enter the Home; I wrote
to the Superintendent and asked him about it.
His prompt reply will ring in my ears for time
and eternity. The letter read, 'Dear sister, yes,
come, *certainly come,*' and closed with the words,
'Your brother.' No words can describe my astonishment. For him to address *me* as 'Dear sister,'
and sign himself as 'Your brother;' it seemed not
of this world, but of heaven. When I arrived in
Chicago, I was met by a missionary and conducted
to the Rescue Home. Oh, the peace and quietude
throughout the whole place! The Holy Spirit
reigned supreme, having entire charge of all. It
was so new, so sweet, and holding out such hope
to all! For the first few weeks I would not have
been surprised to have met Christ face to face in
any of the rooms. I did not say much, but with
keen scrutiny I watched their lives, and if I had
seen a single act contrary to what they professed,
the chances are I would never have been sanctified; but all their practice corresponded with their

profession. Through all the trials and severe testings, they were kept by the power of God."

Sister B—— .was soon wonderfully sanctified by the baptism of the Holy Ghost. She has gone on commanding the respect and holding the confidence of all who know her. She is one of our most trusty and trusted assistant matrons, giving her soul and life to the work of lifting up the fallen. To the God of the Bible be all the honor and glory forever.

LULU L——.

LULU L——, OR FROM DRUNKENNESS TO WOMANHOOD.

LULU L—— furnishes a marvelous exception to all rules in a life of sin and her salvation furnishes one of the most extraordinary exhibitions of grace we have ever witnessed in rescue work. Few have ever gone so low in sin and very seldom has one ever made such rapid strides in divine grace. Her deliverance is wonderful beyond description.

She was an Ohio girl. At eight years of age she was left without a mother's love and counsel and a father's protection. She made a noble fight for a life of virtue and integrity, but the odds were against her. She had no education, and every possible advantage was taken of her. At the age of seventeen she was ruined under promise of marriage.

After she was ruined, she came to the city and for two whole years withstood all inducements to go into a life of open shame. But having once been down, the pressure was too great. She finally sank to rise no more until Christ with His tender touch lifted her from the cesspool of sin to the heights of redemption. By public picnics, theaters, and finally dance-halls, she was led on step by step until she was not only a confirmed drunkard and a public character, but a manager of a house of ill-fame.

At first she drank not so much for the love of liquor, as to keep equal with her associates, but as the steps in sin are always downward, she rapidly grew worse and scores and scores of times was beastly drunk. Her drunken debauches grew in length and her appetite for nicotine became almost vicious. For months at a time she would not draw a sober breath. Her iron constitution stood the strain of this awful life for more than a dozen years, while the average life of a woman in sin is less than half that time.

She had no more than crossed the threshhold of Hope Cottage when the Holy Ghost put her under pungent conviction for sin. She did not have to be converted to abandon sin. She gave up rum and tobacco and turned her back on a whole life of wickedness several days before she was saved. She says: " I never desired rum or tobacco from the hour I entered the home." Hear it, you church members who are still using the weed, waiting for light or more conviction. Remember if you are not convicted for the use of tobacco, is it not because your heart is harder than was hers? She was not only shown that it was wrong, but she was delivered from the appetite and all desire for them was taken away before she was converted at all. Brother, do you not see that if you still use the weed, you are not as far along as a convicted harlot, for she gladly gave it up. She says: " I hate rum and tobacco."

Thank God she is not only saved but sanctified, healed, and living a most beautiful, exemplary Christian life. The grace and power of the gospel has so changed, subdued, and mellowed her life that she is a benediction to all who come under her influence. What a miracle of heaven! What an exhibiton of divine grace!

I call on every one who shall ever read these lines to aid me in giving glory to God for the wonderful display of His power and matchless mercy. Praise the Lord.

MINNIE, NOW ASSISTANT MATRON OF A RESCUE
HOME, AND " DODO."

MABEL, HER RUIN AND REDEMPTION.

MABEL —— was born in ——, Ill., of Methodist parents, and brought up in a Methodist Sunday-school — a bright, beautiful child, furnishing sunshine and good cheer to the home, and making fine progress in school. Her form was slight, but well shaped; her face was innocent, beautiful and attractive. Reared in a country home, she had known nothing of the ways of sin. But before she was sixteen, she was permitted to keep company and buggy ride late at night with one who robbed her of her virtue and ruined her for life.

If this well-dressed brute had cut her throat from ear to ear, and covered her body with leaves in some lonely wooded spot, it would have been a great kindness compared with robbing her of her virtue, smirching her fair name, and leaving her with the burden and responsibility of being a mother, when she was only a child herself. Father, suppose she was your daughter! Mother, what if she were your darling? How would you then feel toward those who are ever planning the ruin and overthrow of innocent girls?

Mabel came to us at Rest Cottage in Chicago, a poor heart-broken and discouraged child, knowing nothing of salvation. O, what a scene! Words can never portray the sorrow and anguish of those awful days. We satisfied ourselves that she had never consented to her terrible ruin, and before God had never really lost her innocence or virtue, and yet she is the victim of a shame that will last for all time. In convulsions of grief and floods of tears, she says: " I must ever be treated as if I were guilty."

What a grewsome, dark side there is to sin that the world will never forgive.

But how transcendently glorious it is to know that we have a Christ who will gladly go out of His way to forgive and forget the darkest sins ever committed, when approached by a penitent soul. It was not long after she entered Rest Cottage until the dear child found the Saviour. It was easy for her hungry, broken heart to yield to the touch of love, and it was His greatest delight to spring to her side, blot out all her sins, comfort and sustain her as only a divine Christ can do.

Her name may never be found on the tablets of Christian fame, but it is carved deep in the hand of the compassionate God of Love. By her beautiful spirit and Christian life, she has imbedded herself in our affections forever, and as missionaries and gospel workers, we shall never cease to love and stand by her.

Beloved, if she were your daughter, you would never ask the question again, " Does Rescue Work pay? "

To Father, Son, and Holy Ghost, be all the glory forever.

TEXAS REST COTTAGE, PILOT POINT, TEXAS.

BERTHA AND ESTHER — THE TWIN SISTERS.

BERTHA and Esther Huling are twins. Their parents died when they were very young, and they were placed in an Orphans' Home. When they were only five years old, a man sixty years of age took them from the orphanage and raised them for shame. He ruined them both before they were women. When he saw that Bertha at the age of thirteen was going to become a mother, the scoundrel put them on the train at Ozark, Ark., and sent them to Denton, Texas, where they were put off the train, thinly clad, penniless, helpless, and friendless.

A holy woman found them in the street, the picture of forlorn despair. Our missionaries went after them, and saved them from drifting into a house of shame, by bringing them to Texas Rest Cottage, at Pilot Point, Texas. Bertha was blessedly converted to Christ the first night, and Esther very soon gave her heart to God.

It was my unspeakable pleasure to be in their company and hear them testify to the power of God to save. If our Texas Home had never done more than to save those beautiful children, it would pay us a thousand times over. But many are there who have been wonderfully saved and sanctified, and a number have been healed through the prayer of faith. Praise the Lord.

REST COTTAGE, CHICAGO.

A SALOONKEEPER'S DAUGHTER.

To save one daughter such as the subject of this sketch is well worth all the money expended since the movement was launched. She is in her nineteenth year, and can not remember when she did not drink strong drink. Her father was a saloonkeeper, and whisky was like water in her home. Her mother died when she was nine years old, and she soon found herself in the hands of a heartless stepmother. At the age of eleven years she was forced out into this cold world to earn her own living among strangers. She sometimes tried to do right; but her earnings were taken to support others who were living in sin, and she received encouragement from no one.

Though she knew nothing of the way of salvation, she at one time determined to reform; but when she came home and declared her intentions, some of the family made sport of it, and her stepmother used such abusive language and called her such vile names that she turned away and went to drinking harder than before to drown her sorrow. She went from bad to worse, and was imprisoned time and again. At one time she spent five months and five days in the workhouse. It was here she acquired the habit of cigarette smoking.

In the workhouse she was sick three months, four days unconscious. The family were notified, but they refused to come to see her, but said she might go to hell. Their written message was so horrific and inhuman that the authorities refused to let the poor girl know the worst. She went in an unmanageable character, she came out far worse. She spent her eighteenth birthday in the workhouse. The last three months before she came to Rest Cottage she paid $120 in fines, obtaining her money without work. The last four weeks before she was found in the police station she had not drawn a sober breath. Now that is enough of the dark side of her life, and it is with a sigh of relief that I turn to the bright side of her story. The moment she crossed the threshold of this homelike " Home," new hope sprang up in her soul. It was only a few hours until she gave her heart to God and was gloriously converted.

In her regeneration all sinful desires and all acquired unholy appetites were taken away except two, a thirst for drink and a desire for dress.

For the past four months she has been a great joy and comfort in the Home. A few times she failed to control her temper, but in the main, has lived a beautiful, exemplary Christian life even before she was sanctified wholly. She has returned stolen money and articles of jewelry, has written twelve letters at a time making wrongs right, knowing, too, that some of her confessions might send her to the state's prsion, she fearlessly told it all. It is wonderful how grace has removed all traces of sin, and her face is radiant with heavenly light.

Since leaving the Home she has married, and we are assured that she is faithfully doing her part to make home happy and life worth living. God bless her forever.

Come unto me, all ye that labor and are heavy laden, and I will give you rest. Take my yoke upon you, and learn of me; for I am meek and lowly in heart; and ye shall find rest unto your souls. For my yoke is easy, and my burden is light. Matt. 11 : 28–30.

MYRTLE.

MYRTLE was the daughter of a Christian minister. Her father died when she was four years of age. The support of six children, three of them very small, fell upon her grief-stricken mother. When Myrtle was eight years old, she was sent to live with a married sister. With but few advantages, she grew to womanhood. At the age of thirteen she was forced out into this cold world to earn her own living. Being industrious and ambitious, she worked hard, returning home only once a year. In 1903, broken in health, she visited a relative in Texas. When convalescent, she was induced to take a position as a companion to a lady who was an invalid. It was here she met the honored member of the Y. M. C. A. who proved her ruin. He was much older than she, consequently she had almost no conversation with him. She says: —

"One night I said my prayers as usual, and fell asleep like the innocent child I then was. How can I tell of that awful moment, when this man, crazed by drink, rudely awakened me from that childish slumber. The memory of it can never fade from my mind. I wept, pleaded, and even prayed, but to no avail. He told me that if I called for help, they would never believe me, and powerless in his strength, I was degraded, robbed of my virtue, and left in hopeless despair, desiring only to die.

"For five weeks I was delirious almost all the time, and my conscious moments were indescribably awful. Once I took morphine, thinking to end it all, but God interfered, and I woke to the bitter knowledge that I was still in this world."

When she was able to be moved, she was sent home to her mother. She had succeeded in burying her sorrow in her own heart. Soon observing she was to become a mother, and determined to hide her disgrace from her people, she left home and wandered from place to place.

As she was walking down the street in Texarkanna, Brother F——, a rescue missionary, read the lines of trouble in her face, and asked if she was not in distress. At first she denied it, and he, apologizing, was about to pass on, when he felt strangely led to turn and speak to her a second time. And almost before she realized what she had done, the secret which she had concealed from all others, was told out to him.

He insisted on her going to our Rescue Home, but her pride resented the suggestion. When he had charged her if she ever needed assistance to write to him, he passed on. It was not long till he heard from her, and he wired her a ticket. But again the devil aroused her pride, and she returned it. Such a war as was waging in her mind! Her sorrow-stricken heart was fairly reeling under the awful load.

That same day she met her betrayer, and told him her situation. The villain, anxious to cover his own shame and infamy, promised to protect her. She boarded at a first-class place, and kept up the deceitful part of a young lady on a vacation, until at last her early training, prompted by the Holy Spirit, asserted itself, and she resented the vile suggestions of this professed Christian. She said to herself and to him, " I have never willingly degraded myself, and I never shall." Here she was thrown under the direst conviction. She lay on her face all night long, weeping, and saying over and over, " If God is just, why has He permitted me to be disgraced without my consent, and exiled from all my people? " Despite the protest of the one who should have been willing for her to do right, she determined to find God if possible, and came to the Rescue Home. She says, " When I entered the Home, and Sister Miller took me in her arms and I laid my weary head just where I used to rest it on mother's shoulder, I would not have left the Home for millions of money. God wonderfully saved and sanctified me. In about three months my precious little one was born, and in one short week God took her from my arms to His beautiful home in heaven. Now that my darling is in heaven, I have only Jesus to live for."

This noble, brave girl is making a valiant soldier of the cross, and is battling for God and souls. I am not ashamed of the gospel of Christ, for it is the power of God unto salvation to every one that believeth. Praise the Lord.

FOUR MISSIONARIES.

"PETE'S PLACE"— A LOW DIVE.

PETE'S PLACE is one of the most notorious dives in the precincts of sin on the West Side. His saloon, or barrel house, has a brothel in the rear, and an opium den in the basement. To approach this place at high noon is not without danger; for here murders are common. It has been said they average about one a week; but it is about midnight when our missionaries come into this haunt of vice and crime. A number of poor unfortunate girls are crouching in the rear of this dark, dismal den. In their midst is a woman, the most prominent figure in the company,— no, not a woman, one who has drifted through stratum after stratum of the vilest society, until she has reached depths of sin, degradation, and crime, where womanhood is entirely forgotten.

As soon as the missionaries approached the little group of girls, this vicious character came rushing to them, and struck one of them in the stomach with her clenched fist, then with a wild look, rushed madly to the other one, and gave her a stunning blow in her face. The saloonkeeper and his wife sought to appease her anger, and avert her assaults, but she was not easily turned aside from her purpose. There can be no doubt but that just here an unseen presence stepped in and protected the lives of those missionaries of the Cross.

They were not frightened, and did not turn from their purpose, but after talking salvation to the girls, and distributing some tracts and gospel papers among them, they felt led to take hold of one drunken girl, and take her bodily out of this den of sin, and this they did under the most ferocious protest of this angered woman. She followed them to the door, and did all in her power to prevent their rescue of this poor girl.

They assisted the unfortunate specimen to the elevated station; they literally dragged her up the stairs, and into the train, where they found the car filled with Nabob passengers of Oak Park, who were returning from the late theaters. She was intoxicated just enough to furnish sport for the passengers, who were inclined to make the most of the occasion. But when one of the missionaries passed about among them, gave out the booklet called, " Four Sermons on Hell," told them about the Rescue Home, and about what they were doing for such unfortunate women, the crowd soon sobered down.

Mary (for that was her name) lodged in Rest Cottage, soon sobered off, and was gloriously saved. This is what we call pulling people out of the fire, and again we glorify God for the grace and power of the gospel in the slums.

JULIA.

JULIA.

THE strange and thrilling story of the life of Julia is almost unbelievable. But we have satisfied ourselves that it is all true, and much more than we shall attempt to record. She was first to enter Hope Cottage as a guest.

When it became known to the citizens of Mount Auburn, of Cincinnati, that the property now known as "Hope Cottage" had been purchased to be used as a home for erring girls, our enemies were enraged, and an injunction was placed on the property to prevent our opening it. Never will I forget the first time when I prayed with this homeless, friendless girl. It was while we were waiting for the trial to come off, or the lifting of the injunction. We had no place for her except a little corner curtained off in one of the large rooms, then the dining-room of the Bible School.

No such institution can ever be launched without facing regiments of living foes. We felt the energy of the Holy Ghost urging us on to disregard the restrictions, and open and dedicate the home. The day was set, the doors were unlocked, and Julia entered this place of blessing. From the hour the doors were opened the place has been one of great grace, power, and glory. If the injunction was ever lifted, I have never been so informed, but the power and glory of God has been so great and the success so phenomenal with this restriction hanging over us that I would be afraid to ask for its removal.

Julia was born in Springfield, Ill. Her father was not only a notorious drunkard, but vicious and brutal in his family. She was the youngest of five children, and was often frightened by his cursing and fighting, and sometimes shooting or using a knife. When she was four years old, her mother, her only friend, was seized by a fatal sickness, and, on account of the drunkenness and abuse of her father, she was taken away from home and then buried by strangers. Julia grew up without education, and felt most keenly the loss of her mother. In her father's drunken sprees he seemed determined to take Julia's life, and it was often with great effort he was restrained.

As she grew up, she was often without shoes or decent clothing. He would mortify the poor girl by compelling her to wear her stepmother's old shoes, which were very broad, and entirely too large. When but a child of thirteen or fourteen, she was compelled to go out and do heavy washings for a living. She was a strong girl, and would wash and iron all day for fifty cents, and at night she would be so tired it seemed she could hardly get home, and then only to be cursed and abused by a drunken father. She went on in this way until her health gave way, and she became a great sufferer. She could no longer do heavy work, and, discouraged and heart-broken, she said, " I must make a living."

Nothing seemed to open to her but a life of sin. She deplored such a life, and her whole being revolted from it. But what was she to do? There was no one to lend a helping hand; there was no one even to advise her, or care what she did. It was thus she was forced into the paths of shame. She had inherited from her father an appetite for strong drink, but did not know it until she had taken her first glass, which aroused her slumbering appetite and fired her whole being with a burning thirst which could not be satisfied, and was never absent until three years ago, when Jesus saved her and took away all unholy appetites.

When once down, she was soon smoking and drinking to awful excess, and though she had a horror for the brothel, and during the fifteen years she spent in sin she had her own private rooms, and never went on the streets to solicit patronage, or even dressed in an immodest way. The gaudy attractive attire worn by sporting girls generally was distasteful to her, and no one would ever suspicion from her appearance that she was living in sin. Her visitors were all known and well-respected business men, generally married men, and often with an excellent wife and grown daughter at home. This awful condition of things is coming into practice more and more, and is now very common. She seldom received strange callers, never unless they appeared as perfect gentlemen, but the steps of sin are always downward, and Julia soon became a confirmed drunkard, and for ten years she was hardly ever sober, day or night.

When she was not too much intoxicated, she was under conviction for sin; but this only added to her torment, for she did not understand it until after she was converted. She was without any knowledge as to how to get saved. She would weep and groan and wish a thousand times that she was dead. She finally came to Cincinnati, and was five months in a sporting house. She underwent serious operations in the hospital at least four times, and when she would go on the table she would be so in hopes that she would die in the operation that it would make her really happy. She knew she would go to hell, but she felt so sure that hell was not so bad as the life she was living that she longed for the change. When she would return to consciousness, she would be so discouraged that she would be for days filled with sadness. This repeated over and over, she determined to kill herself by drinking, and many a time she would drink until she was unconscious, with the hope she would die intoxicated.

After spending many a night in an unconscious state, and always coming out greatly disappointed, she determined to commit suicide by drinking poison. She was drinking in a saloon when the thought seized her that this was the opportunity. She ran across the street to a drug store, secured morphine, and swallowed it before any one discovered the object she had in view. She was soon unconscious, and fell on the sidewalk as dead, and was carried into a house, supposed to be a corpse. But it was discovered there was still life in her body. Those in charge used such means as threw her into paroxysms of vomiting, and next morning at eight o'clock she returned to consciousness, greatly to her dismay and discouragement.

When she would walk the streets, merely to pass a church would put her under such conviction that she would cry and wring her hands, and sometimes almost go wild. At the age of twenty-five she was married, but her husband was worse than a brute, and would club and beat her until he was arrested again and again. Sometimes he would beat her almost to death; she would be weeks recovering from her injuries, and yet she went on in her drunken career until she reached the place where, if whisky or strong drink could not be secured, the hot water would rise in her mouth, and the torture was something indescribable. It is hardly worth while to undertake to picture the feelings of torment of one who is afflicted with the appetite for strong drink.

The average life of a woman in sin is little more than five years; but here is one with such a strong constitution that she has struggled through almost fifteen years of indescribable anguish and sorrow. When she was brought to us, she was not only soaked with rum, morphine, and nicotine, but her mind seemed impaired, and her will was so weakened that she was powerless almost as an infant.

It was in this condition that Jesus found her, and that God for Christ's sake forgave all her sins. The transformation began at once not only in her heart but in her face and life. The work of Christ has gone on with greater rapidity than did the work of sin, and if her awful black record was a miracle of hell, her present condition is a most marvelous miracle of grace. She has been delivered not only from rum and tobacco, but morphine, and all desire for uncleanness, and is to-day a noble exemplary Christian, and a great benediction to all who are in the home, scattering sunshine to all who come and go.

Her body is so wrecked that she had no desire to get well, and for a long time no one seemed to have faith for her restoration to health. We are told that one lung is entirely gone and the other much reduced. How she lives at all seems a mystery, but she does live and lives beautifully to the glory of God. Her heart is as tender as a child's, and her head a fountain of tears. She weeps over the lost, fasts and prays for the unsaved, and God has made her a real soul winner. Sometimes we have thought the Lord would translate her soon, and then she would recover her strength, and go on working and smiling for the Lord.

Sometime ago she sent me the following message: " Brother Rees, I want you to preach my funeral sermon, and I don't want it like other funerals. I want it to be a praise meeting, and a meeting to give glory to God and the gospel to the unsaved."

The influence of her life and the grace she has manifested during the last two years will be as lasting as eternity itself.

A GROUP OF CHICAGO GIRLS.

A GLIMPSE INTO THE SLUMS.

A Tramp Converted.— Many have thought it
was money thrown away to give a poor tramp a
night's lodging, even if he professed to get saved,
but when a poor, friendless, penniless bum bowed
at our altar there was little in sight to hope from.
A night's lodging cost only ten cents, and with it
a cup of coffee and a roll, so we gave him a ticket.
The next day he hunted work, but found none,
but at the mission he testified to a new-found joy,
which eclipsed all he had ever known. We offered him another lodging, to which he replied:
" I will pay it all back when I get work." The
next day he found work, and on his first pay day
brought the twenty cents to pay for the two nights'
shelter from the cold. From the first hour he has
gone straight on as an earnest Christian. Reader,
do you think this was a poor investment? Have
you your money invested where it brings better
returns?

The saints from all over the land have sent us
tons of cast-off clothing. They come to the Rescue Home in barrels and boxes, and then must be
carried in bundles to be distributed among the
worthy poor.

Clothing Distributed.— Two of our saved young men were aiding the missionaries one wintry day, in distributing the bundles. They each had two large bundles strapped on their backs and a great package under each arm. On attempting to board an electric car with these loads, the conductor said, " You can not get on this car with all that freight," to which the young man replied, " I am taking this to the poor suffering people, and you ought to let me ride." The conductor said: " Certainly, get on here, and when you dispose of what you have, come to my house and I will give you a lot more." So he took the conductor's address, and gained another bundle. Brother, are you dead enough to go along the streets with great bundles on your back for the Lord's poor?

A Prayer of Thanksgiving.—When Jim —— was saved in our mission, he had nothing but rags and vermin. A box of cast-off clothing was opened, and he was soon fitted out from top to toe. They were only such as many of my readers have thrown away, but when the garments were handed him he rolled them up in a bundle and laid them down on the mission floor, and got down on his knees by the bundle and prayed and thanked God for them. It was a most touching sight.

A Sad Death.— Our missionaries failed to find this poor family among the starving and shivering of Chicago. Three little children were depending upon an old grandfather for support. He had exhausted his means and all efforts to secure fuel had failed. It was zero weather, and almost night. A blinding storm was raging. The old man bundled up as best he could and left the shivering little ones in the house while he started down the railroad track to see if he could pick up a few pieces of coal to make a blaze. Blinded by the flying snow, he failed to see the limited express and was instantly hurled into eternity. If some one could have taken them a hod of coal, and have told him about Jesus and His power to save, this life might have been redeemed and the children saved this awful sorrow.

In Danger of Freezing.—A young man who had walked the streets seeking work until it seemed that he would freeze, determined that shelter of some kind he must have. He made just enough of an attempt to rob a paint store to get arrested. In court he said: " It is cold, and I might as well be in jail as freeze to death hunting work." He said to the jury: " It is my first time in jail, but I do not like to freeze." Think of it in a city like Chicago, boasting that she has just expended fourteen million dollars for Christmas presents, and yet thousands suffer with cold and hunger and their souls are perishing for the bread and water of eternal life. Beloved, pray that God may touch the hearts of those who have, that they may give to those that have not, and that He will send more divinely qualified missionaries.

Converted on the Street.—A party of our missionaries were doing midnight work in the slums. They met a young man nineteen years old on the street. They told him about Jesus. Conviction seized him, and they all knelt down on their knees on the sidewalk, and the boy gave his heart to God. A few days later, one of the missionaries was walking the street, when a young man hailed her and said, " Don't you remember me? " " No," replied the missionary, " I do not remember you." " I am the boy that was converted on the street at midnight." He had a job, and was rejoicing in his new-found life.

A Detective Converted.—A detective came down to the mission one night to secure the arrest of a certain criminal. He was a fine-looking gentleman, with a Prince Albert coat and beaver hat. During the sermon, the Holy Ghost arrested him. When the altar call was made, he bowed at the penitent form and gave his heart to God, and giving his testimony he said: " I came in here to make an arrest, but the Holy Ghost has arrested me," and in that one service he was arrested, convicted, pardoned, and set free.

A Fireman Saved.—A fireman of a railroad locomotive came into the mission one night. The power of the gospel put him under such conviction that he fell at the altar, but knew not how to pray. When asked to cry out to God, he said: " I never prayed in my life; I do not know how to pray only that little prayer my mother taught me." We said, " Well, pray that." He prayed, " Now I lay me down to sleep, I pray the Lord my soul to keep; if I should die before I wake, I pray the Lord my soul to take;" and while he was praying that prayer, the Lord converted him, and he rose up and testified to the forgiveness of sins.

LUCY.

LUCY, A WHITE SLAVE.

LUCY was born of religious parents, and reared in a Christian home. Her father and mother loved her fondly. She was a beautiful girl, with fair, clear complexion, rosy cheeks, and hair almost golden. Her life was so guarded that at the age of fifteen she knew almost nothing of the ways of sin, and was ignorant of the wiles of Satan. At this age her parents moved from the Hoosier state to Chicago. As they were in limited circumstances, she sought employment, that she might aid in the support of the family. Her eyes fell on an advertisement in the newspaper, " Girls wanted." She was out looking for employment, and on her way home a man about thirty years old met her on the street, who asked her a number of questions, which she, child-like, answered. Attracted by her beautiful face, he determined to capture her for a life of sin. The villain that he was wore good clothes, was of fair speech, and with flattering words made a number of propositions, all of which she resented; but finally he offered her such inducements and made her such promises of nice clothes and a beautiful home, etc., that she went with him to see the place. He took her to a room over a saloon, where he himself was bartender. When she was once inside the room, the door was locked, and the poor girl was ruined. For two days and nights the child was locked in that room, with nothing to eat except one small steak and a few raw oysters. There were two men who had access to her room, and she had no way of escape. She had not the remotest idea when she went that she was going into sin.

On the third day she was removed to a negro sporting house, and placed in the charge of a negro madam, and was instructed to receive callers, white or black, and turn the proceeds over to the villain who had placed her in this house of shame. He told her if she did not obey his instructions he would shoot her, and thus the girl suffered untold agony.

God must have touched the madam's heart, for next morning she made it possible for the poor girl to escape. As soon as she was out of the house, she fairly ran to an officer and told him her story. She was at once taken to jail, and there held for three weeks. She herself was tried under the charge of running away from home, and then held as a witness against the two men who had ruined her. Five times the child was taken into court and compelled to tell the whole story. The attorney on the opposite side did all he could in cross-questioning her to destroy her testimony, but she told it the same every time, and with such frank open face and clear, firm voice that she won the confidence and sympathy of all the officers. In the fifth and last trial something had to be done with the girl. Just as the judge was giving the sentence to five and one-half years in the reform school, two of our missionaries stepped up and asked the Court to send her to Rest Cottage. The judge first asked a few questions, then said, " Yes, I know that place," and within ten minutes she was turned over to us. Within two days after she entered Rest Cottage, she was gloriously converted to Christ. She wrote to her heart-broken mother that she was saved, and the joy in that home is simply indescribable.

It is truly wonderful what the gospel of Jesus Christ will do. To the Father, Son, and Holy Ghost be all the glory forever. Lucy was most congenial in the home, gave the matron no trouble, and received most remarkable answers to prayer. When she was returned to her heart-broken mother, she bore the impress of heaven upon her face, and the message of salvation upon her lips. She is now teaching a Sunday School class of nineteen scholars.

Let everything that hath breath join us in praising the Lord for His matchless grace, and the marvelous manifestations of power in the rescue and salvation of this precious daughter.

NEW ENGLAND REST COTTAGE, PROVIDENCE, R. I.

THE POWER OF THE GOSPEL.

" I AM not ashamed of the gospel of Christ, for it is the power of God unto salvation to every one that believeth." Romans 1: 16.

We are deeply touched with the words we have just heard (a touching rescue song which has just been sung) ; but my heart leaps with joy when I remember that Christ is able to save from the worst of sin, from all vice, crime, and iniquity of every kind; that there are no cases so hopeless but that this gospel may reach them, and, if they will turn to God, they may be saved. It is man, not God, that grades sin. In the sight of God, sin is sin; and it is awful; and it is all awful. Sin is as black as hell from whence it came. God with His great heart of compassion makes no difference. "We have all sinned and come short of the glory of God;" but He has loved us and given His Son for us, and Christ has laid down His life that we might be saved. This is a great comfort to us in these days when there are so many people and so many nice people that object to the truth, and turn away from the gospel, and do not want to be saved. Thank God, the poor outcast, the hungry, the people that are down and can not get

up, God loves them, Jesus died for them and wants
to save them. It was when I had no one to help me
that God took me in. I used to weep and wring
my hands and run my fingers through my hair
and walk through the woods and look up through
the twinkling stars and wonder and weep and sob
and there seemed to be no hope, but when I
turned to Christ, He saved me; all glory to His
name!

We are greatly comforted this morning to know
that we have a gospel that is able to reach the
deepest depths of sin, vice, and crime, as well as
the highest mountains of pride and rebellion
against God. These are times when God seems
to take great pleasure in saving people that nobody
else would think is worth saving. The Lord is
delighted to take in poor wandering outcasts, discouraged, disappointed as many of us have been.
I remember going to bed many and many a time
realizing if I should die before morning I would
wake up in hell. I supposed this was the only
possible result. I did not suppose there was a
way for a wretched man like me to be saved.
Sometimes I became in a manner contented with
the situation and thought if I was in hell it could
not be much worse than this. I was without God
and without hope in the world, but thank God,

this gospel was preached to me, I heard about the Christ who could save to the uttermost all that come unto God by Him. He saved me, and this is why my life is given to the salvation of others. This is why I seek especially the neglected; the people that other folks turn from and I somehow feel God has called me to give them special attention.   The churches do not care for them and many think they are not savable, but the gospel of my text can reach the worst.

A few years ago I preached in the slums of New York.   One morning there were twenty-eight girls sat in front of me, twenty-six of whom were confirmed drunkards.   I preached this gospel in a very simple way, telling of the love of Jesus and His power to save and twenty-four out of the twenty-eight girls turned to God and seemed clearly converted to Christ.   Where else can you get that proportion of the unsaved to turn to God? You must go to the slums where people are tired of sin to reap anything like a large harvest.

God is moving mightily in these days to pick up anybody that will leave sin and turn to Him. A great deal of time and money is spent on people who do not seem to want the Lord.   There is so much begging and pleading with people to get them to come and seek the Lord and then so much of the religious effort and labor of our evangelists is spent in reclaiming backsliders over and over again. Why do we not push out to where people really want God? I know of places where if you tell them of a Saviour's love, they will break down and cry like children, fall on their faces and ask God for Christ's sake to forgive them.

We ought to find out where God is giving His special attention and go there. Our hearts ought to be so like His, that we will run where He runs and that we will pass by the people that He passes over, that we will lift up people that He is trying to lift. God purposes that we shall select, in these last days, those who will accept His grace, obey His voice, and honor His name forever, and He wants us to steer clear of the multitudes of religionists who do not want Christ, who do not want experimental religion and do not purpose in their hearts to obey God and keep His commandments. My heart goes out to the poor, unfortunate, homeless, fallen men and women, whom Satan is seeking to destroy, for I know that Jesus loves them and God can save them.

You meet a tramp on the street, and many a time there is a heart beneath those rags that is tired of sin; a heart that is discouraged; a heart that wants to know something better. Many of

them have been educated, have filled places of
trust, many of them have been members of respectable families, but they have lost their footing, and
have gone down and down, and if you will go to
the lowest dregs of society to-day, you will find
thousands that came from the best walks of life,
humanly speaking. College-bred men who have
had everything that heart could wish, but they
have gone down and lost all hope. Thank God,
there is a gospel that will save them; there is
power in Jesus Christ, His blood can cleanse
from all sin.

A few years ago I preached in a certain northern city, known for its sin and vice and crime —
a rum-soaked, priest-ridden city. The preachers
met again and again to discuss ways and means
to reach the masses with the gospel. Long,
flowery essays were read, speeches made, and
everything suggested but the real old-fashioned
gospel and nothing was accomplished. In that
city was an old disreputable theater — a licentious, filthy old place that would hold eight hundred or one thousand people; and there was a
drunken outlaw, a man that had been in sin until
his body and mind were wrecked as a result of
every possible excess. He had been in prison
twenty-seven times. The people would have been

glad if he was dead, but he was not considered worth killing. God said, " I will take that man," and he saved him and sanctified him wholly and healed his body and he went and opened that old theater, and cleaned it out, and cleaned it up, and brought in the gospel; and God saved more souls in that old disreputable opera-house than in all the churches put together. These are days when God is moving mightily on the lowest hopeless material. He is making some strange selections. It would seem sometimes that He is taking pleasure in making something out of nothing, that He might show the world what grace can do.

There was a river thief of long standing in lower New York, an awful criminal; everybody dreaded him; nobody seemed to love him. Somehow the gospel got to him, he heard about my text, and he turned to the Lord, and Jesus saved him. He opened a mission in Water Street and from the time the door was opened to this hour it has been a place of salvation. Perhaps there is not a spot in America where more homeless, friendless, penniless men have found salvation than at that place. He preached, and prayed, and sang, and shouted and God blessed him and multitudes turned to the Lord. Strange and pathetic are the stories of that work. He had the gospel of my text. He went a little further uptown and found a saloon, called the Cremorne Saloon, and rented a room beside it and named his mission for the saloon, "The Cremorne Mission." Men smiled; the devil hissed through his teeth; it seemed like child's play for a man who had been a drunken outlaw, to start a mission beside a famous saloon and expect to accomplish anything; but it was only a short time until the saloon was no more and the Cremorne Mission stands to-day and has been a place of the salvation of hundreds and hundreds of souls, not because of any human wisdom or might, but because Jerry McAuley had the gospel of Christ, which is " the power of God unto salvation, unto every one that believeth."

A man staggered into the Water Street Mission who had drunk forty-five glasses of liquor within forty-eight hours, hopeless and friendless. He was a man of brains, was educated, had been a good lawyer in other days, but the devil had dragged him down until he was a wreck, lying around in filth and vermin, drinking and smoking whatever he could secure, homeless and hopeless. But one night he heard the gospel of this text and he said, " Is that so, can He do that for me? " They said, " Yes." He believed in Jesus and God saved him from sin. He soon had a good suit of clothes on

his back and money in his pockets. He soon
opened a mission, and another and another until
he had opened thirty-five rescue missions in
America and saved seventeen thousand drunkards,
because he had the power of my text, " the gospel,
which is the power of God unto salvation."

O beloved, we must not be disheartened. We
must not sit down; we must remember that God
loves this great lost world and He is glad to take
in the lowest of the low. He says there is no difference. The people who live on Fifth Avenue and
the boulevards in great mansions are no more to
Him than the poor tramps and harlots and jail-
birds. He would do just as much for the tramps
and bums and unfortunate girls as those who live
in palatial homes and drive through the best streets
with rubber-tire carriages. My heart is with the
lowest of the low and I have no apology to offer
for being where I am.

Three hundred and fifty thousand fallen girls
in this country in sin,— unnameable sin,— sin that
does not differ in the sight of God from other sin.
There is no difference between the fallen woman
and the fallen man; if any difference, she is the
better of the two. The world brands her with
everlasting disgrace and will scarcely turn a hand
to help her, while the scoundrel who ruined her

is allowed to go free and is often welcomed into the society and homes of respectable people. I want to say that the gospel of Jesus Christ does away with all this nonsense and gross injustice. Sin is sin wherever you find it, and unless the sinner repents, he is lost forever.

While preaching in the slums of New York, one of my frail little sisters, who at the age of twenty-six had spent thirteen years in street life, stepped up to me and said, " Brother Rees, I feel somehow that I ought to open a shelter for fallen girls. My few friends have discouraged me, not one of them has given me any encouragement." I knew God had saved and sanctified her and healed her frail body; I heard her story and then slipped into her hand a little offering and said, " Open up a home in the name of the Lord and trust Him to supply the needs." She went down into what was then known as Mulberry Bend and opened two rooms with some pallets of straw, some soap-boxes and some broken stools; no beds, no chairs, no bureaus, no furnishings, just an old rickety table and a few things like that; but the place was packed with girls. At that time I was making regular visits to the slums every fortnight. When I returned, my sister came to me and said, "My two rooms are filled and more girls want to come." "Well," I said, "take more room in the name of the Lord." She took more rooms, got some more straw, some more soap-boxes, and broken stools and packed the place full of girls and salvation. When I returned in two weeks more, she said, " Brother Rees, I have got to have a house." I said, " Take it in the name of the Lord." She took a whole house and furnished it and packed it full of girls and salvation and that was the way one of the most famous shelters for fallen girls was opened. No committee of a dozen women in their silks, no board of trustees. It did not take much money to rent the rooms and it took less to furnish them, but the girls were there and Jesus was there and they found salvation.

God is, in these days, reaching to the uttermost corners of the earth to save the poor, unfortunate people. I can say with the venerable old apostle, " I am not ashamed of this gospel, and I am not ashamed of my Christ, and I am not ashamed of the fish we catch; many of them, it is true, have been unfortunate and have been down very low, but when they are saved and filled with the Holy Ghost, they are going to rank with the best of society in heaven.

Only two years ago I was preaching in a cer-

tain district of one of our western cities and there
strolled into the meeting a discouraged, heart-
broken, hopeless man and sat down away back by
the door. I did not know him, but God loved
him and there was a gospel to save him. He
threw his head down on the back of the bench
in front of him and wept freely. He had been
converted only a short time before, but had had
so little to encourage him and nobody seemed to
be his friend and he was hopelessly discouraged.
Finally, he came forward to the altar. Little did
I know what there was in him. He was the most
notorious burglar perhaps in the Mississippi
valley. There was not a rogues' gallery in the
country without his picture. At the age of thirty-
five he had spent twenty years behind prison bars.
All the detectives and officers of the land knew
him. I did not know him, but God knew him
and reclaimed and blessed his soul that night. A
few days after, he came to the altar and received
the baptism with the Holy Ghost; but though
saved and sanctified, how could he get employment? Nobody, much, had confidence in him.
Thank God, there was a sanctified lumber-dealer
in the city. He said, " I will give him employment." Think of it. A burglar, a thief, an outlaw. Yes, sanctified people will trust men when

nobody else will. He gave him employment. A few weeks later I was in the city and went around to the lumber yard. I said to the employer, who is a personal friend of mine, " How is ——? " He said, " Of the twenty men in the yard, I have not one more trusty." After he was saved, the policemen would meet him on the streets and say, " Hello, ——, what religious dodge is this you are trying to give us? We know you, and it won't be long before we will have you back in jail." After he had walked straight for eight months, one day he was walking through the streets of Cincinnati when a detective and two policemen stepped up to him and said, " Hello, ——, we have been watching you for these eight months and we believe in you, and if you will go with us up here to the rogues' gallery, we will ask them to take your picture out." Well, it made but little difference to him, but he went with them and they took his picture out and in a few weeks he heard they had taken it out in Indianapolis, St. Louis, Chicago, Louisville, and all through the Mississippi valley, because the power of my text had saved him from all sin. There are no hopeless cases, God is able; I wish we might give Him a chance. A few weeks ago I was passing through Indianapolis and ran down to the lumber-yard.

I found my friend foreman of the whole gang of the shipping department. He was giving orders and they were being respected as if he had never been behind bars in his life. He has since married a beautiful sanctified girl and recently I have been honored with one of the greatest privileges of my life, that of breaking bread in his Christian home, a veritable heaven on earth. I do not know when I have been so blessed. Glory to God, forever.

In speaking of the work of lifting up the fallen, people say to me, " O, it does not pay." I want to say to you, there is no investment that pays as well. If people would put their time and strength and money in getting the Gospel to those who are down instead of spending it on dead churches where they do not want the gospel, they would reap far greater results in the salvation of souls. I hardly feel comfortable in steeple houses any more, in too many cases they do not want salvation. It is in outside places, the highways and hedges, the people who are hopeless and helpless, who are hungry for God.

In the city of Chicago, God put it on our hearts to open a Home for fallen girls. A place for them to rest and get saved and receive the Holy Ghost and begin life over again. We took our offering in August and on the first of October, we opened the Home. It would probably have taken a church board two years for careful deliberation and discussing of plans to raise money, but when the Holy Ghost gets hold of any matter, it does not take Him long to make it a success. It is truly wonderful; we are careful to give Him all the glory. Our business is to pull men out of the fire and to save women from sin and from hell. There is in the slimiest slums of Chicago a solid block of sin, one-half a mile square, in which there are two hundred and forty-one saloons, besides brothels, dance-halls, low-grade theaters, etc., and only one little chapel, or place of worship.

The other day we decided we would give the poor hungry men a dinner. So we bought a thousand fresh buns, made a thousand cups of coffee, secured a barrel of apples and other things in proportion and spread a table. Most of the people do not believe in feeding tramps; they are afraid to give a man a meal or a poor old worn-out garment, for fear they will give to somebody who is not worthy. Beloved, I would rather help a dozen that are not worthy, than to fail to help somebody that is worthy and is needing assistance. The dinner only cost us about thirty-five dollars in cash, and at the close of the day, there were seven men who had been gloriously saved. Some of them testified it was because of the extended kindness of the saints. One man said he had not believed in religion before. There has been a stream of salvation in that place ever since. There were seven souls for thirty-five dollars. Can you invest money in these aristocratic churches and have it bring results like that? In many of them there have been thousands of dollars spent with not a single soul saved. Five dollars a head is not expensive for souls, though sometimes we get them at the rate of one dollar each. When you and I come to the judgment and see things in the light of eternity, we will wish we had put more money where it will count for God and souls.

Well, on October 1st, we opened the Home with five or six rooms and in the midst of much opposition. The devil is sure to butt against anything that there is any real good in, but the first year, we rescued and sheltered about fifty girls. If the Christian people were awake to this work, we might give almost everybody a chance, but few know the real condition of things in this country and fewer know the power of my text. Thank God, " it is the power of God unto salvation to every one that believeth." I could give you touching incident after touching incident, I could tell

you things that would make you cry, but that is
not enough, that is not just what we are after; we
want to get conviction from God. We want to
know that God is moving on us in these days in
the rescuing of perishing souls. Down in the
slums of Chicago, there are people who have not
a pound of coal in the house; people are just dying
for food. Right here in Chicago in the midst of
plenty, where people boast of expending nineteen
million dollars for Christmas presents, the poor
are starving for bread, and when somebody starves
or freezes to death, the notice of it occupies about
three lines in the newspaper and the world hurries
on to hell.

The other day I was in the Harrison Street
Police Station and I found a man in a filthy cell
who was arrested for stealing two lumps of coal,
perhaps neither weighing more than five pounds,
and his wife and children were shivering with
the cold. Men steal their thousands and on
account of the rottenness of politics and municipal
government no arrest is made, but the poor are
oppressed and are becoming poorer every day.
The poor are practically without a gospel.

The aristocratic churches do not want these
people, even after we get them saved and sanctified. In Chicago we have had to organize a

church where these would be welcome and where
the best pews are opened to those who have been
among the lowest.

We found a starving family of five in the Harrison Street Jail. They were shipped from Alabama to Chicago. You know how states quarrel
over their poor; nobody wants the poor; Alabama
did not want them; Chicago did not want them, so
they were thrown into the witness cell of the Harrison Street Police Station, all sick and all starving. The hospitals did not want them, they will
not take people unless they are nearly dead, the
county refused them; they were Germans, but the
German consul would do nothing for them. We
took them Thanksgiving day as a Thanksgiving
present. God let us furnish them a home. One
of the children was too near gone and after two
weeks went to heaven. The others recovered and
were grateful for the kindness. How I thank God
that we could care for that little child the last
three weeks of its life and that it did not die in
that dingy cell. And yet thousands are dying in
the dingiest and dampest corners of this earth, not
only without food and raiment, but without the
gospel and without hope. Beloved, my whole
soul is in this work. I want no more Thanksgiving
days after the old fashion — the self-centered, self-

ish way of gathering a few of our friends together and stuffing stomachs, and neglecting the poor. I prefer to go down and eat with the bums and tell them of a Christ who can save to the uttermost. Beloved, I can ask you one or two questions that ought to enable you to determine how Christ-like you are in your life. Who eats at your house when you have a feast? Who eats turkey on Thanksgiving or Christmas in your home? When there is a birthday or anniversary feast, who is it that sits at your table? Who did Christ say should eat with you?

Are you living a Christ-like life? God help us and give us the compassion that He had and let us possess and practice the spirit that He manifested in His work. Some day we will look back and remember our trials and pains as nothing and rejoice that we were ever counted worthy to suffer shame for His name.

FAITH COTTAGE, ASHEVILLE, N. C.

LITTLE H——.

LITTLE H—— is not yet sixteen years old. She was born of godless parents and reared in a home where beer was on the table as far back as she can remember. Her father was always intoxicated and very abusive in his family, her mother a moderate drinker, and the whole household without any knowledge of salvation. Scolding, quarreling, fighting,— the home was a miniature hell on earth. Reader, is it any wonder to you that girls reared in such homes go astray? Are you sure you would have done better under such circumstances? I wonder if you appreciate your Christian homes and training as you should?

Before she was fourteen years old, her virtue was gone and she was in unnameable sin. She never found any pleasure in this life of sin, but a combination of circumstances forced her to it. Men would take her into rooms and force her to drink. She would feel so badly afterward that she would lament and weep over her sins, but there was no one to offer relief. There were scores ready to drag her down, but not a man to lift her up.

She would resolve that she would break away from this life. She would go and get housework to do that she might make an honest dollar, but again and again her hopes were blasted and there was none to help. How the poor child needed some one to tell her about Jesus Christ and the power of His gospel to break and cancel the power of sin! She went from bad to worse until one night she met a girl friend of hers, who was not much older than herself, but more experienced in sin, who was beastly drunk and all that night they reveled in sin and shame.

Next morning they felt so badly that they decided not to go back to their employment. Under the influence of strong drink and nicotine, the devil suggested to them to do some thieving. They stole a guitar, gold ring, and a revolver and found a young man who consented to pawn the articles for them. They spent the day in sin and disposed of about all the money. As evening came on, they knew it would not do to go home, so they took shelter in a house where they thought they would not be found. But late that night a messenger came for them. They jumped out of a back window and ran around through and across the railroad tracks and among the box cars and thus made their escape. They found an old empty house and crawled into it and slept until morning.

H——— had heard of the Rescue Home, but she knew but little about it, except that it was a place where poor lost girls could stay. She knew the direction and that it was two or three miles from where they were, but did not know how to find it. But they were determined to make a search and when they were in the immediate neighborhood, they inquired of the post-man who guided them and they were soon standing at the door of " Rest Cottage."

The door was opened and they came in. No one is ever refused at " Rest Cottage " even if they have to sleep on the floor. They tried hard to get saved and confessed all but their thieving; they so dreaded the penitentiary that this they tried to cover. But, of course, they could not find salvation with sin covered any more than can you, my dear reader.

In about two weeks an officer came and arrested and put them in jail. They lay in jail from Thursday until Tuesday afternoon. They were called into court at least four times during their stay in prison. Our missionaries stood with them in the court room and pleaded for their release in the name of the Lord. On the fifth day the judge turned them back to us. Never were girls more delighted and soon gave themselves over to the Lord and found real salvation.

H——, who is the subject of this sketch, has since been sanctified wholly and went to the Bible school for better preparation to tell poor lost girls the way to salvation.

Beloved, it is truly wonderful what God is doing for these poor girls. All glory to His name forever.

PICKING COAL.

CHRIST IN THE SLUMS.

ON Pacific Avenue, there stands an old leaning, unpainted, dilapidated house. Newspapers were in the windows instead of glass; no carpet on the floor, no table, and not a whole piece of furniture in the house. The furnishings consisted of a small rusty shop stove, an old half bed, broken and ready to fall; and two broken chairs. The pantry consisted of an orange box standing on end, containing three or four cracked dishes. The only articles of food in the house was a third of a loaf of stale bread. On the rickety bed was a woman not less than fifty years of age. The ragged mattress was indescribably filthy, and everything presented the most unhappy and distressing appearance.

The family consisted of a helpless old woman, with her hands and feet all drawn out of shape with rheumatism -- brought on by exposure to cold and wet, while earning her bread by the sale of newspapers on the street, and two little boys.

The older child secured their only means of support since his mother's sickness by selling papers at the corner of State and VanBuren Streets, earning from twenty to forty cents a day.

The younger boy was cook, nurse, and general housekeeper. He slept with his sick mother on the half-bed, and Ben, the newsboy, slept on a cot which was out in the kitchen, but which he was forced to bring into his mother's room every night on account of the great hungry rats that had taken possession of the old shed.

Ben had brought home thirty cents the night before, and Jimmie had bought a loaf of stale bread, and a couple of pork chops such as you can purchase in a butcher shop in the slums. By the use of the last pound of coal, the little cook had fried the chops not more than half done, and that was all the boys and sick mother had had to eat that day. The third of the loaf of bread she had ordered saved for little Ben when he came home hungry, in case he had not had a good day with his papers.

The woman had been a Roman Catholic, but a missionary had given her a copy of the New Testament, and while reading it she had been gloriously converted to Christ. Her spirit was all aglow, and her face was radiant with heavenly sunshine. I have never seen so much contentment, happiness, and sunshine in any room so dark and destitute as I found here.

There was not a single complaint; no trace of

murmuring; she was satisfied with everything; and was praising the Lord continually.

The hovel was owned by a Catholic priest, and the rent had been two dollars and fifty cents per month; but when he heard that she was reading a Protestant Bible, he sent the agent to say that the rent would be six dollars per month.

We prayed, wept, and shouted as best we could under the circumstances, but our shouts choked us, and we felt that on our part, practice would be more appropriate than preaching or shouting. You know now what would come next. The bed and bedding were fired to the dump; the place was renovated, fumigated, and irrigated. The missionaries who were once filled with pride, bought pails, soap, and brushes, and then laughed, wept, and shouted while on their knees scrubbing that miserable filthy floor.

They were so blessed in their souls that they felt they would be glad to scrub another one. This is a part of what the power of the gospel does in the slums. All glory to the Christ who entered and transformed that hovel into a little heaven.

He that is without sin among you, let him first cast a stone at her.   John 8:7.

B——.

B——·· is one of our first trophies in the Rescue Work. She was born and brought up in Virginia. Her parents both died when she was very small. By a noble struggle she resisted sin and maintained her virtue till she was twenty-one years of age. Then, through the most adroit means, she was ruined by a relative. When she had taken her first misstep, all of her kinfolks turned her down with emphasis.

Although it was one of them that led her to the slaughter, they all positively refused to recognize her in any way. They did not even answer a telegram when she was thought to be dying. No one seemed to care for her, and there was no place to go. The door to a life of sin is always open, and the broad road to hell offers many inducements, and makes many promises.

When once started down, how rapidly their feet take hold of death. It is not far from a home of purity and peace, to the morgue, the potter's field, and a nameless grave. Forty-six thousand of these girls fill unmarked graves every year, and since forty-six thousand are going to the potter's field this year, forty-six thousand pure, strong, healthy girls must march up to take their places.

Think of it, parents, where are the forty-six thousand girls to come from next year? And forty-six thousand the year following? They must come from somewhere. They will most of them come from the country and country villages; many of them from Christian homes and the Sunday-schools. I ask you to look at this dark procession marching to the altar almost a thousand a week, just like the cattle march down to death in the stockyards in Chicago. What if some one is solicited from your home? What are your feelings? What is your attitude? And let me ask you, are you doing your whole duty in the protection of the virtue of our youth? Are not the foregoing facts enough to arouse the sympathy, and start the slumbering conscience of the people of American Protestantism?

B—— was drafted into this great army, and had to go. The rigor of the service no pen can describe. The pain and anguish it is impossible for us to conceive. It was only through the gospel that she was brought out of this worse than Egyptian bondage. This was her only fire-escape from a burning hell.

Soon after coming to the Rescue Home, she made several vigorous attempts to get saved, but she made the mistake so common of misrepresenting the situation. These poor girls have been so cast off and put down by everybody that it seems almost impossible for them to believe that we will forgive and love them if they will tell us the worst. So they often cover their lives in part, and are loth to confess their real name. Her child was in her arms, but she represented she was married, and that her husband had deserted her.

But with sin covered, she could never get an experience that would stick. It was an awful struggle, and almost killed the poor girl; but when she had confessed it all out, and sent home some things she had stolen, and confessed to a woman, with whose husband she had lived in sin, God gloriously saved her.

Let me diverge enough to say that this crime among married men, and even among church members in high standing, is becoming terrifically alarming. It was this married man, a church member in good standing, who brought her to the city, and after some weeks deserted her; and has doubtless gone on ruining and deserting others. God in heaven open the eyes of parents to the dangers of these awful times! Is it not time that the pulpit was thundering out a Sinai gospel of hell and eternal damnation for all such satanic hypocrites?

The dear girl has gone on beautifully in her Christian experience, and feels heart-broken as the time approaches when she must go out to make her way in this friendless world again. It breaks our hearts to part from these precious girls, who have been saved and transformed until their natures seem almost angelic, but they must go to make room for others.

Thank God! She does not go out alone. The Holy Spirit will go with her, and a host of true friends will follow her with their prayers. Praise the Lord.

REST COTTAGE, NO. 3, GREENSBOROUGH, N. C.

PEARL — A MARVELOUS TRANSFOR-
MATION.

ONE wintry November night, the wind was blowing and the snow flying, when a beautiful young girl of nineteen stood at the door with a six-weeks' old baby in her arms, seeking shelter from the storm. She was not only a sinner, but so possessed and so completely controlled by the devil, that nobody could live with her. Her ungovernable temper made her unmanageable. She had been in one or two Rescue Homes, but they could do nothing with her. She would not only break up the furniture, but break up the folks if they did not get out of her way.

Our doors are open to such girls day and night. She was given a warm welcome, and kindly treated. She was very soon found on her knees, weeping over her sins. As is common, she came to us with a string of lies on her lips, but under conviction, she confessed that she had never been married and gave her correct name. One confession after another was made, and wrongs were righted, until at last God forgave her sins and wonderfully saved her soul.

It was not long till she was seeking the baptism

of the Holy Ghost, and when she unconditionally gave her all to God for time and eternity, He gave her the blessing in her heart and she was unspeakably happy. The glory of God filled her soul, and the shine of heaven was on her face. How the complexion of everything in her life was changed! No more fits of anger — no more slamming doors or knocking over chairs — no more hard words or angry looks. All was changed to the placidity of grace and heavenly quietude.

Pearl soon found employment in a public laundry. Before she went out to work, she had said to me, " I feel called to missionary work, and want to go to the Bible School for preparation." I had sent a number of girls to school, but some way did not feel led to give her much encouragement in that direction.

The first time she came home from her work, she said, " Brother Rees, I have seventeen dollars laid up for paying my way to the Bible School." I said, " That is good," but did not yet say much; but I found that she had been tithing her income and had bought Bibles, and given to the other girls in the laundry.

When she came home a second time, she said, " I have twenty-five dollars toward my support in the Bible School." By this time I saw there was good mettle in her and said, " That will be enough; go and get your outfit, and I will take care of the rest."

Please note the power of the gospel. That sinful girl, almost insane at times with inflamed anger, boisterous, and most aggravating in her manner, entered the Bible School and lived a most exemplary life for a whole year. The following is the testimony of her room mate, given at the end of the year: "I have lived with Pearl all this school year; have seen her under the most trying and provoking circumstances; I have never heard an unkind word fall from her lips, or seen her when her spirit was the least ruffled." This is one of the miracles of the gospel in the slums. Praise the Lord.

DELLA.

RESCUED FROM AWFUL SIN.

DELLA —— is twenty-one years old. She was born in a typical Methodist home in the State of Alabama. She was brought up religious, but without salvation. At the age of fourteen she was ruined under the promise of marriage. The villain was a married man, though he had concealed this fact from her. When once ruined, every door to sin and perdition was wide open to her. Under the promise of ease and luxury she was induced to go into a house of shame. Here she was assigned a room and compelled to pay twelve and one-half dollars a week for her board.

After more than five years in sin, she testifies that nearly all the girls she has ever met have been forced into sin for the sake of a livelihood. In this haunt of vice she was expected to drink with all the company she received. Some have wondered why nearly all the sporting girls become confirmed drunkards. The madams of these houses keep liquor and wine, and gentlemen callers are expected to pay for all the liquor consumed. So the more a girl will drink, the more profit to the madam, and the better she is pleased with the girl. To stand in with her mistress and hold her place the poor girls are almost compelled to drink and smoke.

Della and her sister were in sin in the same house. One day Brother B——, a holiness preacher of Alabama, together with a missionary, went into this house and held a service. When the brother prayed, Della's sister was seized with conviction, and she could never shake it off until she was saved. Ten days after she was converted, the Lord took her to heaven. She went shouting through the gates into the city of gold. What a transformation, from a brothel, from that awful place of shame, to the " Celestial City of Light! "

" Verily I say unto you, that the publicans and the harlots go into the kingdom of God before you."

Before she died she made Della promise to quit sin and get saved. The funeral was on Friday, and the following Sunday Della was gloriously converted to Christ. She came to Hope Cottage for shelter, and was soon sanctified wholly. Thank God she has gone as straight as a string from that very hour. She is supporting herself by honest labor, and praising the Lord for full salvation. She has not the least desire for drink or tobacco and no disposition to go back to the old life. Two more miracles in the slums. O glory to God, forever.

CARL, THE CONVERTED BAR-TENDER.

A CONVERTED SALOONKEEPER.

AND just here I must tell you about the saloon-keeper whose name is Carl, and whose picture accompanies this sketch. He was born in Germany, and came to this country four years ago, at the age of twenty-two. He was a machinist, earning eighteen dollars per week until there came one of those miserable strikes, when he was forced out of employment. He was induced to take the position as porter in a saloon, and was then promoted downward to the position of bartender. And it was there he was standing, dealing out distilled damnation, when Dicie and Anna stood before him and preached Jesus and salvation to him. He had sometimes been under conviction, but did not know what was the matter with him.

One night he was serving the drinks to a man who threw down a twenty-dollar gold piece, and was so intoxicated that he was hardly capable of counting or caring for the change. The change was put on the counter, but the poor man was so overcome that he would take only a couple of dollars at a time, and would stand and talk, and hardly knew enough to care what became of the money. The owner of the dive was present, and winked at Carl to brush the money into the till.

When he saw that his boss wanted him to steal the money, the devil overdid himself, and he said, " That is going too far," and from that hour conviction deepened in his heart, so that when Dicie, who was not yet converted, and Annette, who had but recently been saved from a life of sin, both with Bibles in their hands, stood in that saloon and told the bartender about Jesus and His salvation, and begged him to get down on his knees and pray with them, although he was not ready to take that bold step, they found him fully prepared for their message, and ready to promise that he would come to the mission.

The following Wednesday night he paid a man one dollar and a half to sell whisky in his place while he went to the mission to get salvation. That very night he fell at the altar, and God gloriously saved his soul. With radiant face and blood-washed spirit he stood up and confessed that God for Christ's sake had forgiven all his sins.

He never went back to the saloon, not even for his back pay. He soon obtained employment at his former trade, and a few weeks later was sanctified wholly. He is a living, walking miracle,

getting remarkable answers to prayer, and winning souls to Jesus. He is one of our best street
preachers, and feels called as a missionary to
Japan.

All glory to the all-conquering Christ forever.

Verily I say unto you, that the publicans and the harlots go into the kingdom of God before you. For John came unto you in the way of righteousness, and ye believed him not: but the publicans and the harlots believed him: and ye, when ye had seen it, repented not afterward, that ye might believe.   Matt. 21 : 31, 32.

A MISSIONARY IN A DIVE — TESTIMONY OF J. A. S.

SHORTLY after our Rescue Home in Chicago was opened, I became acquainted with a young girl in the slums. I was very much interested in her. She was a beautiful young girl, but steeped in sin. I lost track of her, and felt led of the Lord to go at midnight, a party of us, to search the slums, and find this lost girl. Our friends told us that such a search was useless in a city of two million people, but what seemed impossible with man was possible with God.

We went about midnight, and for about an hour our labor seemed almost useless. As we were going home I felt God turning me around toward the "Red Light" district, a district where a policeman is scarcely ever seen, and where people hardly consider it safe to walk in the daytime. I was strongly impressed to enter a certain dive, known by all to be one of the very worst dives of the city. I felt like that was the place, opened the door, and walked in, and the party that was with me followed, and there I found the very girl I was looking for.

It would have made your heart almost break to have heard her as she cried out, " O Miss S——,

O Miss S——! Did you come at last to take me away?" And she put her arms around me, and hugged me, and said, "O, take me away from this place, this awful place!" It was a negro dive, and the woman who kept it was a great big negress weighing about two hundred and fifty pounds. Her eyes glowed like flames of fire, and she seemed like the very demon himself, as she saw the girl with her arms around me. In this awful dive only white girls were kept, beautiful white girls, patronized by those awful negroes. The woman said to me, "What do you want, what are you here for? Don't you know what this place is?" I never answered, and God just poured strength into my soul. She said, "You get out of here just as quick as you can. You are here at the risk of your life."

Do you suppose I could have left that place with that young girl hanging round my neck, begging me to save her? *Never!* I made up my mind that the woman would have to walk over my dead body before I would leave without accomplishing the purpose for which God had sent me there. I turned to the negro woman and said, "I will never leave this place until this girl goes out with me." She became greatly enraged, cursed me, and poured forth a perfect torrent of abuse, but I scarcely heard her. The angels were just hovering over, the glory of God filled my soul, and it seemed like I was in heaven itself.

She said to the others who were with me, " You get out of here," and they went out, and I was left alone, after midnight, in that negro dive, but there was not a fear in my soul, no, not one. I believe I felt a little like Daniel in the lions' den; the lions were all around, but the Son of God was standing by me.

Finally the woman said to me, " I see you are not going to get out." I did not answer her; I did not have to; but I turned to her and said, " I want you to go to your wardrobe and pick me out a nice dress and coat and hat, and fix this girl up for street wear." Then I turned upon her, and told her she was on the road to destruction, and was damning the souls of these girls, and dragging them down to hell. God poured the message through my lips, and as dark as that woman was, she actually turned pale in the face. I led the way upstairs and said, " Now you get the clothes to fix this girl up; " and she obeyed me like a little child. We dressed that girl, and got her ready, then we came down where the other girls were, and I said to her, " Now you go around and tell the girls good-by," and I spoke to them of Jesus,

16

and they broke down and wept, and God had right of way in that awful den. I brought that girl to Rest Cottage, and it seemed to me that I hardly touched the sidewalk. I just walked on air. It was two o'clock at night, and there were no street cars, and it was a long way to walk. The girl was black and blue from blows she had received, but there was such hope in her face — she was *going to Rest Cottage.*

By three o'clock she was settled in a clean room, and the next day she gave her heart to Jesus. Talk about rescue work! Does it pay? It pays as no other work in the world pays. These precious girls! When you give them a chance, they never get over it. They never get over the lives of the missionaries. Even if they go back into sin, the prayers of the saints follow them, and are never forgotten.

There were two girls in our Home who had been saved, but the devil was tempting them to go back into sin. We pleaded with them not to go, but the devil was pressing them, and they went. A little later they came back, and said that as they went to open the door of a house of sin, they could hear the wails and prayers of the Christians in Rest Cottage. They could not go in, they could not stand our prayers, and so they came back.

J. A. S.

TESTIMONY OF BROTHER K——.

"WE were looking after the interests of Rescue Work in the Indian Territory. We found a poor girl in the Durant Jail. Her mother had died when she was quite small. She was placed in the care of her brother-in-law, who led her into sin before she reached womanhood, and when he found that the matter was going to bring disgrace upon his home, he turned her out of doors. She had nowhere to go, slept in box-cars, and roamed about from place to place, until finally she landed in the Durant Jail in the month of February, and had to walk the floor to keep from freezing. She was invited to the Rescue Home. The city authorities remanded her fine, and turned her over to our care. When she arrived at the Home, Sister Roberts, who was then matron but has since been called home to heaven, met her at the door, kissed her, and gave her a warm welcome. The poor girl said, "This is the first time such a thing has happened since my mother's death." She was soon blessedly converted to Christ, is earning her living in an honorable way, and is happy in the Lord. Some have asked me, "Does Rescue Work pay?" For six years I have been engaged in evangelistic work, and holding many rescue meetings. It is certainly the most paying work I have ever known anything about, and one which God's special blessing rests upon. During the last year I have seen more than three hundred souls saved or sanctified: have raised one thousand one hundred dollars for Rescue Work, and have had.more money for myself than ever before.   B. M. K.

EVA.

A DONATION.

IN direct answer to prayer, there came a barrel to Rest Cottage sent by express, and prepaid. It was filled with the most beautiful clothes for children and babies. Just what the Home was needing at the time. It also contained a bag of breakfast food, one of dried apples, and nearly one-half gallon of jelly. These had been carefully packed by loving hands, prompted by pious hearts. But the most touching part of all was in the very center of the barrel — a little bag with forty cents in it from a little child, to be used for coal and food for some poor family.

Who can doubt that the Lord hears and answers the cry of those who are in need, and God is always willing to use even a child to bless and help fallen humanity.

There was more gospel in that barrel, and more real piety and devotion in that little bag from that little child, than can be found in many loud housetopped professions in these days. How we need a revival of that kind of gospel for the slums.

And the Spirit and the bride say, Come. And let him that heareth say, Come. And let him that is athirst come. And whosoever will, let him take the water of life freely. Rev. 22: 17.

Now when Jesus was risen early the first day of the week, he appeared first to Mary Magdalene, out of whom he had cast seven devils. And she went and told them that had been with him, as they mourned and wept. Mark 16: 9, 10.

DOES RESCUE WORK PAY?

THIS is the question sometimes raised, but always by those whose hearts are not in the work. We grant that a great deal of the so-called rescue work has failed. Scores of homes have been opened by unspiritual churches, or by some of their members, who are so in bondage to it that they allow it to be held under the authority of the church, and the backslidden minister manipulates all, just as he does in the church, and in a few months it is closed; and the impression is made on the people that the girls can not be held from their lives of sin. O, what a mistake, all for the want of the blessed Holy Ghost! Where He is in charge, failure is impossible. He never knows defeat. All we need is to understand that the battle is the Lord's. There is not one girl in ten in the haunts of shame who is there of choice. Most of them hate the life with a perfect hatred. They would rather be dead, thousands of them, than to go on in a life of sin. But they are helpless; they are down, and there is no one to help them up. They are ruined forever, ruined for everything else.

If a mule falls down in the street, there are

twenty men ready to help him up and give him another chance; but if a woman falls there are twenty people ready to kick her and send her lower.

Thousands of pure country girls are allured into our great cities and led into houses of disrepute through so-called employment agencies. Let me sound a note of warning to the country girls all over the land: Do not respond to the advertisement of an employment agency, though it may be published in your church paper, unless you have some means of knowing that it is a reliable firm.

Three hundred and fifty thousand women and girls in the United States alone are in sin and shame, and most of them brought up in country homes. They do not want to go to church; the churches do not want them. Shall we let them die and be carried to the morgue, fill nameless graves in the potter's field, and be lost forever, or shall we give them the gospel and give them another chance, let them begin life over again, and furnish them a home until they are saved and sanctified, then place them in Christian families, where it will be possible for them to become true wives and pure mothers?

With all the power of my being I repudiate the

idea so often expressed by the words, "The bird with the broken wing can never fly so high again." The sentiment is of the devil. Thank God we have a gospel which can repair all broken wings, broken limbs, broken hearts, broken hopes, broken homes, and wrecked and ruined lives, and make them better than they ever were.

"Where sin abounded grace did much more abound." "And I will restore unto you the years that the locusts hath eaten, the canker-worm, and the caterpillar, and the palmer-worm." O, glory to God, I know it is so. Thank God, we may redeem the time wasted in sin. "All things are possible with God, and all things are possible to him that believeth."

Let me give you a sample. F—— was a bartender, a gambler, a pugilist, and a drunkard. His skill in mixing fine drinks always secured him a good salary, but sin had made him more of a brute than a man, and one Sunday our prison corps found him locked up in a little dingy cell in the Harrison Street Police Station. They preached Jesus to him, but he seemed as hard as a stone. One of our missionaries extended her hand through the bars and pleaded with him to give his heart to Jesus. He ordered her to leave his cell door, but instead she dropped down on the stone floor and wept and wept and prayed to God for him. She handed him a card announcing our services; and to get rid of her he promised her that when his fine was paid he would come to the mission.

He had no thought of keeping his promise, but some days later he was walking the streets and put his hand in his pocket for a piece of tobacco and drew out this card. He remembered his promise, came to the church, and was gloriously converted that night. It was winter and the snow was a slush.

After the service, about eleven o'clock at night, he went back into a dark alley in the rear of the church and knelt down in the snow and said: "O God, this is too good to be true, but if I am really converted and You want me to serve You, take away this appetite for whisky and tobacco." Right there in the snow and water God removed all desire for strong drink and tobacco, and after a year he testifies that he has never wanted it since.

He soon obtained a position with small pay. Liquor-dealers came and offered him large wages. He was working for six dollars a week, and they offered him twenty-two or more to stand behind the bar, but he stoutly refused and always testified that he was saved and that God had saved him from all sin. His ungodly friends did their worst to throw him off the track, but he lived a happy Christian life for eleven months without a break, and then a man who knew him well boasted that he would make him angry. He knew what a fighter F—— was, and that he had a hasty temper. One day he came to where F—— was at work and insulted him. He endured it all like a Christian until the man finally slandered his mother. Like a flash the old man rose up in him, and grabbing the man by the throat with one hand he was just about to strike him with the other, when he remembered that he was a Christian, and he did not strike, but looked at him and said: "You know that if you had talked that way to me eleven months ago I would have knocked you down," but turned away and felt just as badly as if he had struck the man.

He came to the church broken-hearted, and said: "What can I do to get rid of this unmanageable temper?" We had told him about sanctification, but he had been so wonderfully saved he had never felt the need of it. Now he said: "I know what you mean; I must have the experience," and with diligence he sought until he was sanctified wholly.

With what telling effect he stands in the corridors of that old jail and preaches Jesus to the prisoners, pointing out to them the very cell in which he was locked up when the missionaries brought the gospel to him! He never has any trouble in getting their attention, and the effect is most blessed. It is now more than two years, and he is going on, working for the salvation of souls.

ANNA.

CHILDREN IN THE SLUMS.

A Child Missionary.— Lester is thirteen years of age, and is a faithful slum mission worker in the jails and among the fallen. When he was only eight years old, he was the instrument in the hands of God in rescuing his drunken father from a life of sin and shame. Now his father is a Christian worker, and the child accompanies him almost every Sabbath through the jails and among the lost, preaching the gospel of Christ to the hopeless. "And a little child shall lead them."

. . . .

A Child in Jail.— On October 27, I spent some time in a certain Chicago police station. In one of its dingiest cells I found a little boy, perhaps five years old, with his father who was awaiting trial. It was one of those sad cases of a wrecked home and scattered family, and there seemed to be no other provision made for the child. The little fellow had slept two nights on that hard wooden bench without pillow or covering. The father told me that the child was very unhappy the first night, but was settling down to prison life.

. . . .

Wrongs Made Right.— Little Phil, who was not brought up, but just " came " up in the slums, heard the gospel, and was wonderfully converted to Christ. He very soon felt that some wrongs must be made right. The little fellow had been riding to his work of mornings with the engineer on a certain railroad instead of paying his fare; but after he was saved, the Lord showed him that he must make it right with the railroad company. This he was only too glad to do, as his little heart was fairly bounding in the love of Christ.

.   .   .   .

Another Case.— Little C——, a slum urchin, was at the altar seeking the forgiveness of his sins. After praying and weeping for a time he rose up and said frankly, " I can't get religion; it is no use for me to try." Some one asked why. He said, " Well, I have been stealing rides on the electric cars, and every time I try to pray, these things come up."

He was asked if he was willing to make it right, to which he promptly responded, " Why, yes, if I only knew how." " How many times do you suppose you have ridden without paying your fare?" After a moment's thoughtfulness, he said, " I think it was about three times, but to be sure, I'll call it five."

After receiving some instruction he put twenty-five cents in an envelope and sent it to the president of the Traction Company. He very soon received a beautiful letter from the head of the great Union Traction Company of Chicago, commending him for his course. But long before he received a response to his letter, he received a telegram from the Throne announcing that all his sins were forgiven, and he was made unspeakably happy.

.   .   .   .

Cruelty to Children in the Slums.—The power of the gospel not only reaches hardened adult sinners, but ignorant little children are often blessedly and clearly converted to Christ. Little tots who have been trained from their infancy to steal, lie, and deceive, are converted into beautiful little Christians. They have been sent to the saloon for beer ever since they were large enough to carry a quart pail. Some of them have aided in the support of the family by gathering cigar and cigarette butts from the street. But when they are converted, they seem to as instinctively turn away from sin as do those who are older. A little fellow who had been converted at the service returned to his home and said, " Papa, I am a Christian, and I can't gather cigar stubs for you any more," and instantly his father knocked him sprawling across the room.

A little girl said, " Mamma, I have given my heart to Jesus, and I can't go to the saloon for any more beer," and immediately she was beaten and bruised in a most cruel manner. In some cases parents have been so abusive that their children have had to be taken from them. But in almost every case these little folks stand true to Jesus.

Little Anna was at the altar weeping and sobbing one night, when we said to her, "Anna, what is the matter?" She said, " My parents have whipped me, and kicked me, and pounded me, and shut me up in a dark room, all because I was a Christian, until I thought perhaps it would be better for me to give it up; but when I did, I was so miserable that I have made up my mind that no difference how much I am whipped, or kicked, or cuffed, I will stand it all for Jesus if He will only come back into my heart." Of course He came back, and she rose from the altar, her face radiant with heavenly glory.

JUDGMENT IN THE SLUMS.

ONE of our missionaries who had herself been a drunkard for many years, and was familiar with all the haunts of vice and dives of iniquity in a certain great city, was doing missionary work in the slums.

When she entered a saloon which she used to frequent, the new bartender protested against her doing missionary work, and said, " You are going to break up this man's business," and ordered her out of the saloon. She said, " No, I don't want to break up his business, but I want God to do it."

She knew the proprietor well, and watched for an opportunity when he would be in. Entering the saloon one night, she said to the proprietor, who seemed very glad to see her, " Harry, it is all right for me to distribute tracts, and tell the girls in the saloon about Jesus, is it not? "

He said, " Yes, Georgia; I wish all the girls were as you are to-day." He gave her perfect liberty in his place, for he knew so well what she had been, and what a marvelous change the Lord had wrought in her life.

When she was through, Harry followed her, and the missionary who was with her, outside,

and stood on the curbstone and wept like a child
while she preached Jesus to him. She said,
" Harry, you should go back into that saloon and
knock the head out of those barrels, pour out all
that rum, and close up that house."

With great tears running down his face he said,
" I know that is just what I should do." The great
strong, nice-looking man, twenty-nine years old,
stood on the street with streaming eyes, and said
more than once, " I feel afraid to go back into that
saloon." The missionary felt it might be his last
chance, and warned him faithfully. The last thing
he said to her was, " I don't know but I will do as
you say," and she bade him good-night.

As soon as she was gone, he stifled his convictions, or failed in his courage to do what he knew
was right. About a week later he was sitting in
his place of business, his favorite girl, about whom
he and another man had had trouble, was sitting
by his side, when the angered man entered the saloon, and shot him all to pieces, shot him six times
after he was dead. This was clearly the judgment
of God on the place.

The result was, the saloon was closed and three
of the eight girls in the house were sent to the Rescue Home, one of them being the beautiful girl

over whom poor Harry lost his life.   She has since been wonderfully saved.

A further result of this awful tragedy was that the Chief of Police had all the saloons raided and closed, that had girls connected with them.   All these scores of girls were arrested and sent to the House of Detention.   Many of them were girls who had never been arrested before.   Some of them had parents who knew nothing of their whereabouts, and such a scene of weeping and wailing in the prison has seldom ever been witnessed.   The authorities kept sending them to our Rescue Home, until we had seven more than we could comfortably accommodate.

How marvelously the missionary's prayer was answered, that "God would break up the business."

FANNY.

FANNY, THE NOTORIOUS HIGH-LIFE SPORT.

WHAT awful tales of woe are poured into our ears in these awful days of misfortune, vice, and crime! Our hearts are broken again and again, and we sincerely hope that we will never become so accustomed to these stories of sorrow that we will not be deeply grieved and touched with compassion for earth's unfortunate and neglected.

Fanny B—— was born in the Cincinnati Hospital in 1869. She was a legitimate child, but her father was in jail, and there was no other place for her to be born. Owing to trouble between her parents, she was deserted and thrown into the Children's Home.

When twenty-one months old, she was adopted by a whisky dealer who had no children of his own. Being unusually bright, she took to schooling, and was educated, especially in music.

Her adopted father became a professional gambler, and deserted his family entirely. With broken home and broken hearts, Fanny and her foster-mother were forced to support themselves by taking in washing. Some years later he returned and took Fanny's hard earnings, and set up in the saloon business, where he is to-day.

She struggled against awful odds, and maintained her virtue until at the age of seventeen she married a railroad man, and thought to have a good home and live a happy life. But alas! he was not a man, but a villain. The scoundrel soon proposed that her pretty face, fine form, and attractive manners might become the means of their support, and insisted upon her selling her body for bread. It seems clear beyond the utmost stretch of human thought of what atrocious, diabolical men can be capable. How little our pure daughters know what they are in the presence of, when they meet these well-dressed demons in society, many of them appearing most amiable, affable, and gallant, but they are commissioned recruiting officers of hell.

Fanny was soon made acquainted with a number of cattle shippers and wealthy business men. She received one lesson after another in the school of vice and crime, until she became an expert in alluring men with money into attractive haunts of shame, to be ejected from these assignation houses a few hours later without a dollar. At one time she and her husband grew tired of this life, straightened up, moved to another city, and for a time lived comparatively respectable. During this time a beautiful daughter was born to them; but it was not long until his black heart broke over all restraint, and he became a thieving gambler, abusing Fanny until it was impossible to live with him. After threatening her life until she was compelled to appeal to the authorities, he stole the little girl and absconded.

Heart sick, and broken in health, she despaired of life. But about that time a wealthy Kentucky man offered her great inducements to become his mistress. He provided all he promised. He lavished upon her diamonds, pearls, emeralds, and rubies until she fairly glittered. She wore the best gowns that money could buy. He bought her a house of eleven rooms, carpeted and furnished with the best material. Very soon she opened one of the finest houses of ill-fame in all Cincinnati. Everything she touched turned to money, but it was blood money, and was no object to her. Many a time she and Orpha (who was with her for five years at this period of her history), would start out of an evening with a thousand dollars or more in their pockets, and think nothing of spending a hundred of it in a single place, drinking, smoking, and sporting.

At one time her husband returned and robbed

her of more than a thousand dollars' worth of jewels, and stole the daughter a second time. She says, " Then it was I thought I would go crazy." She then drank to excess, smoked cigars and cigarettes, took morphine and cocaine, and often tried to take enough to make her sleep forever. But the hand of God held her on earth, and she would awake to awful disappointment when she found she was not dead.

While she was madam of a high-toned house of shame, owned her own property, and run her own saloon, her house was patronized by high-toned church members, wealthy married business men, who had beautiful wives and grown daughters at home, who spent their money in this way.

Her husband drifted to Little Rock, and married another man's wife while he was away from home. The husband coming home, in a rage, overpowered him and killed him with his own revolver.

Excessive drinking caused Fanny to lose her house, fortune, and business. She says: " I positively know that for five years I drank from one quart to three pints of whisky every day, besides wine, beer, and mixed drinks:"

Readers, listen: That beautiful woman drifted from that palace with all its elegance, from diamonds, rubies, seal skins, and elaborate and expensive gowns, down and down, until she became a common drunkard. She is not able to tell the number of terms she served in the workhouse. She went lower and lower, until she was a common beggar in the streets. She sat up many a night in bar rooms, and for a whole week at a time would not have a bed. Tired, sick, and starved, she did not have a cent. She was arrested time after time, till the officers and judge were tired of seeing her. But let *her* speak a moment: " When I had plenty of money, running an open house without license, I was never arrested. Every month I went around to the saloons, and paid the whisky bill of all the policemen who traveled our district, and as long as I would do that, I was never molested."

It was when she had reached the bottom in poverty and degradation, while begging whisky in a low-grade saloon, she was found by her old friend and comrade, Orpha, who has been saved from a life as dark as Fanny's, but who is now a missionary of the Cross. She was brought to the Rescue Home, where she very soon turned to the Lord, and sought salvation. Her testimony is as follows: " Well, praise the Lord! Glory! Glory! Glory! Praise Him for His wonderful kindness to me.

He has lifted me out of the pit. Glory to His name forever! I praise Him for answering prayer. I want to learn enough of God's Word to preach the gospel to my fallen sisters." To God be all the glory forever.

ELLA.

LITTLE ELLA, OR FROM THE OPIUM DEN TO THE SACRED DESK.

LITTLE Ella, the subject of this sketch, was born in an Iowa country home. It seems that nature was all against her. Her disposition was contemptible from a child; no one could live with her in any satisfaction. She was a natural liar, and it seemed she could hardly tell the truth. Her mother died when she was five years old. She was whipped and abused by a stepmother, and was utterly without moral or religious training. She can hardly remember when she began to use strong drink, but became a drunkard very young, and for years was under the influence of liquor whenever it could be obtained.

At the age of fifteen she was sent to Chicago in the company of a Chicago cab driver. She came under the promise of employment with good wages. She knew but little of the world and sin, except as it existed in small country places. She knew absolutely nothing of the dens of vice in a great city like Chicago.

On arriving in the city, she was asked to enter a boarding house as the cab driver's wife. Against this her whole being revolted, but with threats indescribable she was forced to surrender. Against all his satanic assaults she stood out for a whole day and night, but a lonely girl in a strange city, without a friend, having never had the counsel of a mother, the pressure was too great, and she went down.

She was so ignorant of the ways of sin that she did not know it was possible for her to make sin remunerative; she was utterly unacquainted with the consequences of such a life. Having once fallen, it was easy for her to go down lower and lower. She sank until she found herself friendless and homeless in a saloon, where she was kept intoxicated all night long.

A number of times she determined to do better, and made earnest efforts to get on her feet, but with nobody to help, her efforts were in vain. She was finally sold to the keeper of a sporting house for the sum of five dollars, and went from bad to worse until she found herself in one of the lowest opium dens of our great city. There were times when it seemed there was nothing too bad for her to do. She even stooped to hustling in the saloons.

Yet, all this time there was something nobler struggling for supremacy in her heart and life. At one time she was seeking a better way, and walking the streets of the city when she was approached by an old villain whose form was bending with years, from whom she received the vilest propositions. Nobody ever said a kind word, nobody ever talked to her about her soul, she did not know she had any friends.

When her frail body became so weakened by disease that she was no longer serviceable in the haunts of vice, she was carried off to the public hospital. It was here she was found by one who was her real friend, and who brought her to Rest Cottage. Very soon she was gloriously converted, and a little later received the baptism of the Holy Ghost and fire. But the habit of lying had so fastened its fangs upon her that she told one lie after she was saved, which has given the poor girl great pain, and her repentance has been with tears and bitterness. God has touched her sick body, and she has been made a real benediction. She has been instrumental in leading souls to the " Fountain of cleansing," and although through all her earlier years all her natural tendencies seemed to be against her, she is most conscientious, and has come to be a lover of truth, integrity and uprightness, carrying great reservoirs of sunshine wherever she goes, and has been a great benediction to the Home.

After hours of weeping and praying she received what she felt to be a clear call to the mission fields of China. God opened the way, and we placed her in the Bible school. God has made her an efficient preacher of His Word. She is such a Quakeress that she will preach whenever the Spirit comes upon her, whether on the street or electric car or in public parks. One summer afternoon Sister Knapp took the girls for an afternoon in River Park. Public preaching is prohibited here by law, but Little Ella did not know this, and feeling the Spirit of the Lord come upon her, she lifted up her voice and began to preach.

The crowds assembled, the boatman on the river drew up to the shore, and climbed upon the bank to listen. After a time the officer on the opposite side of the park heard her voice, came over, and taking her by the arm said: " See here, you are not allowed to preach in this park." Little Lizzie, who had also been rescued from a life of sin, stood near, and turning to the policeman said: " Is there any law against our preaching to you? " Surprised, embarrassed, and confused, the officer said: " No, I do not know that there is." Little Ella turned to him and finished her sermon. It was a real victory for the gospel.

At the close of her message, a brilliant young Jew stepped up and said: " I have never read your Bible, I have only heard a little. Will you tell me the story from the manger to the cross?" and sat down on the grass at her feet while she told him of the birth, suffering, death, resurrection and ascension of Jesus. His eyes were filled with tears, and he seemed deeply touched.

It is the salvation of such girls as these that encourages our hearts in hard places to push this battle to the gate, and makes us feel that we must rescue others from the same fate. Will not all who read these lines pray earnestly that Little Ella may be made a missionary of the cross, and that the rescue work may be greatly enlarged throughout our borders?

Ten thousand blessings on all who pray for or contribute to this much neglected work.

FEMALE PRISONERS EATING CHRISTMAS DINNER.

RESCUE WORK.

For many years I have felt a strange drawing toward the slums of the great centers of our population. In the spring and summer of 1901, God laid upon my heart the burden of this awful need in this great sin-ridden city of Chicago. Though I met with much to discourage me, I felt an unseen hand urging me to open a rescue home for the fallen girls and women and to secure missionaries to go through the dives and lanes and brothels and fish them out of the cesspools of sin and help them into the " fountain for cleansing."

At camp-meeting at Portsmouth, where I had held camp-meetings for ten years, I stood up and asked my friends to give me fifteen hundred dollars to start a rescue home in Chicago. They granted my request before I sat down, and on the first day of October I opened the home at 1541 Franklin Boulevard, and dedicated it with tears and shouts for joy and victory. A great cloud of His glory settled down on the home that first day, and thank God, it has never lifted for an hour. The home we named " Rest Cottage." The power of God in the home is so great that the girls are often converted before they have been in the house twenty-four hours.

A number of our girls have been called to missionary work; others of them are already real soul winners, and others are in the Bible School in preparation to enter the field, and I believe He will make them mighty soul winners in the very haunts of vice from which they have been taken.

The work in the police stations and jails has been crowned with phenomenal success. What a great joy it is to see beautiful, shining characters standing true to Jesus and preaching to others, who were themselves only a few months since in the depths of sin. How can we expect these poor girls to leave their sporting houses and give up sin before they have a place to go? Some of them have been robbed of their virtue by some murderous villain, and then dumped into a whirlpool of sin and shame. Shall we leave them to die and fill nameless graves and a devil's hell, or shall we take off our gloves and reach down and help them up where they can stand on the " Rock of Ages " and sing the song of redemption?

I was never more certain of any calling than that I am commissioned of Heaven to lift up the fallen and save these friendless, homeless girls from an endless burning hell.

May God abundantly bless the many friends who have aided and contributed so nobly toward this work. They have greatly helped me by their prayers; many have helped by money, clothing, bedding, provisions, etc. God bless every one of them. Tons of cast-off clothing and provisions have come in from all over the country, which has greatly aided the missionary in relieving the suffering among the poor. I wish those who have so nobly contributed could look upon some of the scenes of suffering and sorrow and then witness the joy and childish glee caused by their liberality. My soul revels with the glory of God, and my heart fairly bounds with delight every time I visit Rest Cottage. In no other place am I more blessed of the Lord than in the jails and prisons, preaching and praying with the lowest of the low. I often long for another opportunity.

When I am in Chicago, I scarcely ever fail to spend my Sunday in Harrison Street Police Station. True, I return from these revolting sights sick at heart, unable to eat or sleep, but it keeps me in touch with humanity and a compassionate Christ. I weep over the lost, and my head is a fountain of tears. The world is dying for a more tearful religion. May God keep us tender hearted and enough like our Master to be always moved at the sight of suffering and always ready to bless and help those who are in distress.

RESCUE HOME AT COLUMBUS, OHIO.

A WEDDING IN REST COTTAGE.

THE strange story of Origene and Mable is almost unbelievable. Some real facts read like a romance, and are stranger than fiction.

Mable, a beautiful girl nineteen years old, of German and French extraction, was found by a missionary in one of the barrel houses of the "Red Light" district of Chicago. Without reluctance she turned from the haunt of sin and came to Rest Cottage. She said, "I was brought up a Catholic. My father was a very ungodly man. I was forced to leave school at the age of fourteen, and at fifteen was pushed out into this friendless world to make my own way. Life was a struggle. One year ago I met Origene, who is now my husband. He is in the Marine Hospital, sick with pneumonia. We loved each other, and went to a Catholic priest to be married, but his charges were more than we could pay, so we have lived together without marriage until he grew sick, then I had no place to go.

Origene was of French and Spanish descent; was educated for a Catholic priest. He was ten years in a convent, and wore the robe three years. A number of times he was put on bread and water diet, because he dared to speak to a woman. The last time he was thus afflicted, he leaped from a second-story window, and made his escape. He beat his way to Mobile, and shipped to South America as a cabin boy; from thence to Australia, then back to Liverpool, and on to Boston. He was made steward, and came to the great lakes. When he met and fell in love with Mable, she obtained a position on his boat as second cook, and thus they followed the water until he was taken sick.

Mable was not long in Rest Cottage until she was gloriously converted to Christ, and confessed that they were not married. As soon as he was discharged from the hospital, she preached Jesus to him until he was wonderfully saved from rum and tobacco, all sin, and all desire for it.

He had never prayed, except by the use of Catholic forms, but under Mable's fiery exhortations, he was made to cry out in desperation for deliverance from sin. With trembling voice, and breast heaving with emotion, he prayed through to victory. When the struggle was over, his very lips were white, and his face was radiant with holy joy. His eyes fairly sparkled when he said, " It is all gone." His sins were rolled off of his soul, and his heart was dancing with delight. They said, " Now we want to be married," and the matron, who is also an ordained minister, had the privilege of joining them in holy wedlock in the Rescue Home.

That was a simple but Pentecostal wedding. The power of God was so felt that there was no doubt but that Jesus was at that wedding, and again turned water into wine. It was a time of holy joy. They have both walked in loyalty to Christ, giving faithful testimony of His power to save from all sin.

He said, " I was brought up to a *form* of religion, but never until recently have I known God. I have given up the use of tobacco. At a sailors' meeting, a sailor offered me a cigar. I declined it, and said I did not smoke any more. He replied, ' Your liver must be out of fix.' I said, ' No, I am a Christian. I have quit serving the devil; am now serving God.' "

They are now a happy couple, journeying to the city of God. They may sail some high seas, but they have taken Jesus as their pilot, and the Bible as their chart, and we shall expect to see them sail into the heavenly ports with flags flying high. All glory to God! It is another of the miracles of the gospel in the slums. *Praise the Lord.*

And Jesus said unto her, Neither do I condemn thee: go, and sin no more.   John 8: 11.

TESTIMONY OF ONE OF OUR BEST GIRLS.

DEAR FATHER REES: The Lord has certainly dealt graciously with me, for I have not only sinned greatly, but have sinned against light.

In the first place, God wonderfully blessed me with a Christian mother, one who was not only justified, but also sanctified and anointed with the Holy Ghost fire. When I was but seven years old I got under deep conviction from her godly life, seeing her go about her work with a shine on her face, the praises of God on her lips, and singing the songs of Zion, always rejoicing in the Lord though passing through severe trials.

I was so convicted that I went to her three times and said, " Mama, I want the same kind of religion you have." Each time she knelt down and prayed with me, and one night in the middle of the night the Spirit wonderfully revealed Jesus to me as my Saviour. How I shouted, prayed, and sang that old song, " Blessed assurance, Jesus is mine." I have often said I had a prayer meeting with the angels.

I walked in the light of my conversion until I was eleven, and got under conviction for sanctifi-

cation, and was sanctified and baptized with the
Holy Ghost at home. I saw the vision of an angel
come in at the door, and it seemed the angel just
lifted me up, up above the world, and what power
and glory filled every fiber of my being! How I
shouted and sang, " The half has never been told."

But the night after I was sanctified I joined a
dead, formal church, the members of which did
not believe in sanctification, divine healing, or
saying much about Jesus or this salvation, but said
they believed in just living their religion.

Of course I believed every one that said, " Lord,
Lord," were the saints of God, and entered the
church all on fire for God, and for the church,
too. They thought me very peculiar because I testified in the midweek prayer meeting the year
round (for the young workers in the church never
testified, only in the revival meetings, when especially urged by the pastor). But I had real salvation, and could not keep the good news to myself. I became more puzzled all the time trying
to agree with the church members, because when
I read the Word of God it plainly taught me
things they did not believe in, and condemned
things they did, and yet they were doing the work
of God, and when they died expected to go sweep-
ing through the pearly gates to glory.

I often heard the minister bring in Hebrew and Greek when preaching, so sometimes I would think perhaps I could not understand the Bible because I did not understand Hebrew and Greek.

So by trying to agree with these church members I began to compromise, and therefore was overcome, and lost the grace of God out of my heart, became disgusted with churches and church people, and quit going to church. Having other things to discourage me, and having a longing for something to satisfy my soul, and seeing others seemingly satisfied with the pleasures of the world and sin, I determined to try and find a satisfying portion there, and plunged into sin and worldly pleasure.

I found Satan a hard task-master, and how he bound me to sin. I got into trouble, brought disgrace to myself and family, but was determined if I could not run away and hide it all from my mother and folks I would take my life. But God began to lead me otherwise. I had no one I could or would go to in my trouble, so unworthy as I was, I began pleading with God, and repenting of my sins.

I will never forget how I felt when I first realized I had lost the joys of my salvation. One evening my mother asked me to sing some songs about living in the land of Canaan and being baptized with the Holy Ghost. I sang them, but there was no response in my heart, and no glad hallelujahs welling up in my soul.

I had never heard of the Revivalist people, but a lady gave us one of the papers, and I saw the picture of the two Rescue Homes in it. I wrote them, asking if I could come to one of the Homes, and they answered kindly, saying for me to come. When I entered the Home I was thrilled with joy to see the young women (as missionaries) singing, shouting, praying, weeping over lost souls (even fallen girls), preaching, testifying on the streets, everywhere talking about Jesus and the glad tidings of great joy. I felt I had been right, that I had understood the Bible aright, and that it was for the young as well as the old to give up all worldly and carnal things and enjoy this full salvation, and be firebrands for God. My conviction began to deepen; indeed, I felt as if I were on the very brink of hell. I took a Bible, got on my knees, and prayed the very prayer David prayed when he had sinned against God, and longed for the joys of His salvation to be restored unto him. I felt I needed some one to pray with me, so I asked God to put it on one of the missionaries to come and help pray me through, and He sent Miss

Stromberg. So one morning at morning prayers Miss Stromberg began praying for me, and how I wept over my sins for they seemed to rise as mountains. But the ever-loving, compassionate Saviour heard my cries, and they all disappeared in the fountain. Miss Stromberg sang,

> "Blessed quietness, holy quietness,
> What assurance in my soul."

And indeed it was so. I felt I just wanted to be real quiet, and have nothing disturb that blessed, holy quietness.

Soon after I was sanctified, felt clean and empty, but the Holy Ghost did not come in until after I came home. Bless the Lord, "the Lion of Judah broke every chain, and has given me the victory again and again."

Then saith he to his servants, the wedding is ready, but they which were bidden were not worthy. Go ye therefore into the highways, and as many as ye shall find, bid to the marriage. So those servants went out into the highways, and gathered together all as many as they found, both bad and good: and the wedding was furnished with guests. Matt. 22 : 8–10.

MAY JENSEN.

MAY was left motherless at two years of age. Adopted by a Danish family, she had moral training and ordinary church privileges until she was thirteen years old, at which time her own father allured her from her foster home with promises of a pleasure trip to Denver, fine clothes, etc. He was the first to rob her of her purity, and then force her out into a life of open shame. How atrocious and diabolical! It baffles all imagination. She secured a position as waitress in a restaurant, and thought she would do better, but the position, with its attending evils, only threw her with questionable associates. She changed her name as often as she changed places, that her brutal father might find no trace of her. Her life of shame went on from bad to worse, and she became a hard drinker. In her testimony she said, " I have tried everything in the way of sin." She served several terms in the city workhouse. After four years of this life, her frail body gave way under the awful strain, and she was taken to the city hospital sick with pneumonia. After a severe illness she was discharged before she was fully recovered. With no other place to go, she returned to the haunts of shame, but being no longer a source of revenue to the managers there, she went to the Humane Office, and was returned to the hospital. She said, " How I longed for friends, for some one to help me, but there was no voice to comfort, or no hand to help." It was at the hospital that she heard of Rest Cottage, and a missionary brought her to the Home. Her poor, emaciated body was only a shadow of what had once been a beautiful girl; her large dark eyes and her wavy black hair were still beautiful. Her clothing was not suitable for the ragbag, her body covered with vermin, and her frame bending with the load of sin, she sighed for deliverance. The very next morning she was blessedly and consciously saved during prayers. Her life from that hour gave clear evidence of transition from death to life, and she never once doubted her acceptance with God. She always referred to her past with great sorrow. Her physical suffering increased as the days went by, but her marvelous faith held her as a cable to the " Rock of Ages."

She was very happy amid all her sufferings. It was soon apparent that she was rapidly approaching the end of her earthly stay. On the twenty-ninth of March, in a fainting condition, she was so near the heavenly shores that she gazed on eternal realities, and saw the angels coming for her; but later when she revived she told the matron that they refused to take her. This gave the matron great concern, for she knew that they were only waiting for May's sanctification. She read the Word, and prayed with her, and in a day or two, May had the clear witness to her entire sanctification. She said, " Why, I did not know that God could take all sin out of our hearts." Previous to this it was with difficulty that she spoke, but now with supernatural strength she praised God for about an hour. Her decline was gradual, but on April 20 she was taken much worse. In her paroxysm of pain, her submission to God was beautiful. All day Friday her life hung in the balance, but visions of rapture from the glory world bore her up in her hours of extreme pain, and she would often exclaim, " Jesus wants me; I am going to be home with Jesus. I am so glad I *know* He will take me; I want to see *Him* first of all." She often tried to sing, " I am nearer, drawing nearer." She was very appreciative of all that was done for her. At midnight she put her arms around the matron's neck and exclaimed, " Oh, Sister M——, what would I do if it were not for you; you are so kind. And little Anna, too." (Little Anna was one of the girls in the Home who so patiently waited on her.) She would often say, " I am not going to stay long, and I am ready to go." Sister

F—— was reading to her the twenty-third Psalm, and May repeated with her, " Yea, tho' I walk through the valley of the shadow of death, I will fear no evil; Thy rod and Thy staff, they comfort me." Then when she came to, " Thou anointest my head with oil, my cup runneth over," she repeated it with heavenly unction. Her heart was burdened to the last for the lost girls in the slums.

While one of the rescued girls was praying, little May, without a struggle, breathed her last, and slipped away to be with Jesus. Like the afterglow of a beautiful sunset, the glory of God lingered long in the room, and the radiance of the skies fell back on her beautiful, silent face. Thank God! She has passed beyond the foul touch of Satan to where sin, sickness, and pain are never known.

The funeral was held at Rest Cottage, and the rescued girls were the pall-bearers. What a sacred sight to see her sisters from the slums bearing her body to a Christian burial. How different from a funeral in the potter's field! It was a most touching occasion, and the power of God was over all.

What a Christ! What miracles of grace! Think of it — from the cesspools and sewers of vice and crime to a place on the best boulevard in the heavenly city.

THE NEEDS OF THE WORK.

First. We need twenty-five more thoroughly qualified and equipped slum missionaries. They must be thoroughly consecrated, and fire-baptized. They must be willing to suffer all sorts of self-denial, and lay down their lives for the lost. You can hardly imagine the perils of the slums. Besides, they are exposed to all sorts of vermin, and every contagious disease known to the climate.

We need at least two hundred and fifty dollars a year for the support of each missionary, and even then they have to practice great economy and self-denial. With tired feet they walk many a long walk when five cents for car fare would relieve the situation. Brother, sister, have you ever thought what a glorious privilege it would be if God would allow you to support a slum missionary? To have a representative preaching the gospel in the slums and pulling souls out of the fire. What a reward in Heaven for every soul saved. While you are asleep at midnight she is going through the dives, brothels, barrel-houses, and joints, telling the sweet story of Jesus and His power to save from sin. Beloved, at least pray about it, and ask God to send us the needed means.

Second. There are two of the Homes we ought to buy. They are offered very low, and if we are unable to buy them, it will not be long until we will have to move. For this we need ten thousand dollars ($10,000). Will all who read this report, pray earnestly that God may touch hearts and provide the means?

Third. Our funds for relieving the worthy poor are entirely exhausted. Our missionaries have a remarkable capacity for making a few dollars go a long way among the poor. For three cents they can give a family of hungry children a loaf of bread, and it is worth many times that to see them devour it. For fifteen cents they can furnish a hod of coal which will keep them from freezing through the night.

We have used tons and tons of cast-off clothing, and are able to use an almost unlimited quantity. Some have asked us to say what is needed or what we could use in the Homes. We can use anything that you could use in your home. Provisions, bedding, table linen, toweling, and everything that is used in a home will be thankfully received as from the Lord.

FORM FOR PLEDGE.

Believing this rescue movement to be of God, and desiring to aid in saving the fallen, I hereby promise to give within one year the sum of

.... *Dollars.*

$............Date..................190

Name.............................

Address............................

" Give and it shall be given unto you." Luke 6: 38.

" He which soweth sparingly shall also reap sparingly." 2 Cor. 9: 6.

" He that giveth unto the poor shall not lack." Prov. 28: 27.

Money to be sent to —

SETH C. REES, 533 N. PINE AVE., CHICAGO.

THE IDEAL PENTECOSTAL CHURCH

By SETH COOK REES

One writer says, "It is a treatise on the characteristics and qualities of the Pentecostal Church, i. e., that part of the Church which has received her Pentecost. Our author writes not as a theorist but as one who, having received the baptism with the Holy Ghost and fire, has proven himself 'a workman that needeth not to be ashamed,' and has witnessed under his own ministry the striking characteristics of a Pentecostal Church. In putting this book before the public he seeks only the glory of God." This book sets forth the qualities and characteristics of the real New Testament Church in seventeen chapters, together with a half-dozen sermons and the author's experience.

CONTENTS

FROM MANY TESTIMONIALS WE SELECT A FEW:

W. B. Godbey: "The Pentecostal Church, by Rev. Seth C. Rees, the fire-baptized Quaker, is a Niagara from beginning to end. It is orthodox and full of experimental truth and Holy Ghost fire. You can not afford to do without it. I guarantee you will be delighted and electrified from Heaven's batteries."

Christian Standard: "It is safe, sound and evangelical, uncontroversial and admirably adapted to circulation among all believers."

Michigan Christian Advocate: "He writes in a sweet and attractive spirit. We could wish it a wide circulation."

Religious Telescope: "It is written in clear, nervous English and glows throughout with the evangelical fervor of its author."

Rev. George Hughes, Editor of the Guide to Holiness: "I like it; it is square out, and that suits me. It ought to have a good sale."

Rev. John M. Pike, Editor of Way of Faith: "The book glows and burns with Holy Ghost fire, and has stirred our spirtual being to its very depths."

T. J. Hoskinson: "A faithful presentation of the truth. There is nothing better in print."

L. Milton Williams: "I know of no other man in the holiness movement, whose books and preaching have been of more blessing to my own soul than those of Brother Seth C. Rees."

Price, Postpaid, 50 Cents. Four Copies Postpaid for the Price of Three. Special Rates by the Quantity

SETH COOK REES

533 North Pine Avenue.   **CHICAGO, ILL.**

FIRE FROM HEAVEN

By SETH COOK REES

This book does not indorse wildfire, or strange fire, but holy fire — the only fire that will destroy formality, worldliness, and carnality.

One brother writes : " ' Fire from Heaven ' is truly inspiring. *Fire* is always fresh. A fire is ever the same, and yet always changing ; so with this book ; it is fresh, every line, and will greatly refresh the saints who enjoy *full salvation*. It holds the Spirit's freshness from first to last."

Rev. John Pennington says : " The books that bless us are those that grip us like a vise and will not let go. Those that ' grapple the mind and produce conviction ; the conscience, and produce contrition ; the will, and produce resolution.' Such are ' The Ideal Pentecostal Church ' and ' Fire from Heaven,' by Evangelist Seth C. Rees."

Over 300 Pages. Price, One Dollar. Four Copies Postpaid for Three Dollars

CONTENTS

1. Fire from Heaven.
2. Established in Christ.
3. God's Choice of Instrument.
4. Stephen's Fulness.
5. The True Saint.
6. Rooted and Grounded.
7. Abounding Grace.
8. The Secret of the Lord.
9. Exploits.
10. A Larger Outlook.
11. Abundant Resources.
12. More than Conquerors.
13. This is That.
14. The Holy Peace.
15. Call of Rebecca.
16. Blessings in Disguise.

SPECIAL RATES TO AGENTS

SETH COOK REES

533 North Pine Avenue.   **CHICAGO, ILL.**

TITLES in THIS SERIES

geles, 1925), *AROUND THE WORLD BY FAITH, WITH SIX WEEKS IN THE HOLY LAND* (Los Angeles, n. d.), *TWO YEARS MISSION WORK IN EUROPE JUST BEFORE THE WORLD WAR, 1912-14* (Los Angeles, [1926])

6. Boardman, W. E., *THE HIGHER CHRISTIAN LIFE* (Boston, 1858)

7. Girvin, E. A., *PHINEAS F. BRESEE: A PRINCE IN ISRAEL* (Kansas City, Mo., [1916])

8. Brooks, John P., *THE DIVINE CHURCH* (Columbia, Mo., 1891)

9. RUSSELL KELSO CARTER ON "FAITH HEALING." R. Kelso Carter, *THE ATONEMENT FOR SIN AND SICKNESS* (Boston, 1884) *"FAITH HEALING" REVIEWED AFTER TWENTY YEARS* (Boston, 1897)

10. Daniels, W. H., *DR. CULLIS AND HIS WORK* (Boston, [1885])

11. HOLINESS TRACTS DEFENDING THE MINISTRY OF WOMEN. Luther Lee, *"WOMAN'S RIGHT TO PREACH THE GOSPEL; A SERMON, AT THE ORDINATION OF REV. MISS ANTOINETTE L. BROWN, AT SOUTH BUTLER, WAYNE COUNTY, N. Y., SEPT. 15, 1853"* (Syracuse, 1853) *bound with* B. T. Roberts, *ORDAINING WOMEN* (Rochester, 1891) *bound with* Catherine (Mumford) Booth, *"FEMALE MINISTRY; OR, WOMAN'S RIGHT TO PREACH THE GOSPEL . . ."* (London, n. d.) *bound with* Fannie (McDowell) Hunter, *WOMEN PREACHERS* (Dallas, 1905)

12. LATE NINETEENTH CENTURY REVIVALIST TEACHINGS ON THE HOLY SPIRIT. D. L. Moody, *SECRET POWER OR THE SECRET OF SUCCESS IN CHRISTIAN LIFE AND*

WORK (New York, [1881]) *bound with* J. Wilbur Chapman, *RECEIVED YE THE HOLY GHOST?* (New York, [1894]) *bound with* R. A. Torrey, *THE BAPTISM WITH THE HOLY SPIRIT* (New York, 1895 & 1897)

13. SEVEN "JESUS ONLY" TRACTS. Andrew D. Urshan, *THE DOCTRINE OF THE NEW BIRTH, OR, THE PERFECT WAY TO ETERNAL LIFE* (Cochrane, Wis., 1921) *bound with* Andrew Urshan, *THE ALMIGHTY GOD IN THE LORD JESUS CHRIST* (Los Angeles, 1919) *bound with* Frank J. Ewart, *THE REVELATION OF JESUS CHRIST* (St. Louis, n. d.) *bound with* G. T. Haywood, *THE BIRTH OF THE SPIRIT IN THE DAYS OF THE APOSTLES* (Indianapolis, n. d.) *DIVINE NAMES AND TITLES OF JEHOVAH* (Indianapolis, n. d.) *THE FINEST OF THE WHEAT* (Indianapolis, n. d.) *THE VICTIM OF THE FLAMING SWORD* (Indianapolis, n. d.)

14. THREE EARLY PENTECOSTAL TRACTS. D. Wesley Myland, *THE LATTER RAIN COVENANT AND PENTECOSTAL POWER* (Chicago, 1910) *bound with* G. F. Taylor, *THE SPIRIT AND THE BRIDE* (n. p., [1907?]) *bound with* B. F. Laurence, *THE APOSTOLIC FAITH RESTORED* (St. Louis, 1916)

15. Fairchild, James H., *OBERLIN: THE COLONY AND THE COLLEGE, 1833-1883* (Oberlin, 1883)

16. Figgis, John B., *KESWICK FROM WITHIN* (London, [1914])

17. Finney, Charles G., *LECTURES TO PROFESSING CHRISTIANS* (New York, 1837)

18. Fleisch, Paul, *DIE MODERNE GEMEINSCHAFTSBEWEGUNG IN DEUTSCHLAND* (Leipzig, 1912)

19. SIX TRACTS BY W. B. GODBEY. *SPIRITUAL GIFTS AND GRACES* (Cincinnati, [1895]) *THE RETURN OF JESUS* (Cincinnati, [1899?]) *WORK OF THE HOLY SPIRIT* (Louisville, [1902]) *CHURCH—BRIDE—KINGDOM* (Cincinnati, [1905]) *DIVINE HEALING* (Greensboro, [1909]) *TONGUE MOVEMENT, SATANIC* (Zarephath, N. J., 1918)

20. Gordon, Earnest B., *ADONIRAM JUDSON GORDON* (New York, [1896])

21. Hills, A. M., *HOLINESS AND POWER FOR THE CHURCH AND THE MINISTRY* (Cincinnati, [1897])

22. Horner, Ralph C., *FROM THE ALTAR TO THE UPPER ROOM* (Toronto, [1891])

23. McDonald, William and John E. Searles, *THE LIFE OF REV. JOHN S. INSKIP* (Boston, [1885])

24. LaBerge, Agnes N. O., *WHAT GOD HATH WROUGHT* (Chicago, n. d.)

25. Lee, Luther, *AUTOBIOGRAPHY OF THE REV. LUTHER LEE* (New York, 1882)

26. McLean, A. and J. W. Easton, *PENUEL; OR, FACE TO FACE WITH GOD* (New York, 1869)

27. McPherson, Aimee Semple, *THIS IS THAT: PERSONAL EXPERIENCES SERMONS AND WRITINGS* (Los Angeles, [1919])

28. Mahan, Asa, *OUT OF DARKNESS INTO LIGHT* (London, 1877)

29. THE LIFE AND TEACHING OF CARRIE JUDD MONTGOMERY Carrie Judd Montgomery, *"UNDER HIS WINGS": THE STORY OF MY LIFE* (Oakland,

[1936]) Carrie F. Judd, *THE PRAYER OF FAITH* (New York, 1880)

30. THE DEVOTIONAL WRITINGS OF PHOEBE PALMER Phoebe Palmer, *THE WAY OF HOLINESS* (52nd ed., New York, 1867) *FAITH AND ITS EFFECTS* (27th ed., New York, n. d., orig. pub. 1854)

31. Wheatley, Richard, *THE LIFE AND LETTERS OF MRS. PHOEBE PALMER* (New York, 1881)

32. Palmer, Phoebe, ed., *PIONEER EXPERIENCES* (New York, 1868)

33. Palmer, Phoebe, *THE PROMISE OF THE FATHER* (Boston, 1859)

34. Pardington, G. P., *TWENTY-FIVE WONDERFUL YEARS, 1889-1914: A POPULAR SKETCH OF THE CHRISTIAN AND MISSIONARY ALLIANCE* (New York, [1914])

35. Parham, Sarah E., *THE LIFE OF CHARLES F. PARHAM, FOUNDER OF THE APOSTOLIC FAITH MOVEMENT* (Joplin, [1930])

36. THE SERMONS OF CHARLES F. PARHAM. Charles F. Parham, *A VOICE CRYING IN THE WILDERNESS* (4th ed., Baxter Springs, Kan., 1944, orig. pub. 1902) *THE EVERLASTING GOSPEL* (n.p., n.d., orig. pub. 1911)

37. Pierson, Arthur Tappan, *FORWARD MOVEMENTS OF THE LAST HALF CENTURY* (New York, 1905)

38. *PROCEEDINGS OF HOLINESS CONFERENCES, HELD AT CINCINNATI, NOVEMBER 26TH, 1877, AND AT NEW YORK, DECEMBER 17TH, 1877* (Philadelphia, 1878)

39. *RECORD OF THE CONVENTION FOR THE PROMOTION OF*

SCRIPTURAL HOLINESS HELD AT BRIGHTON, MAY 29TH, TO JUNE 7TH, 1875 (Brighton, [1896?])

40. Rees, Seth Cook, MIRACLES IN THE SLUMS (Chicago, [1905?])

41. Roberts, B. T., WHY ANOTHER SECT (Rochester, 1879)

42. Shaw, S. B., ed., ECHOES OF THE GENERAL HOLINESS ASSEMBLY (Chicago, [1901])

43. THE DEVOTIONAL WRITINGS OF ROBERT PEARSALL SMITH AND HANNAH WHITALL SMITH. [R]obert [P]earsall [S]mith, HOLINESS THROUGH FAITH: LIGHT ON THE WAY OF HOLINESS (New York, [1870]) [H]annah [W]hitall [S]mith, THE CHRISTIAN'S SECRET OF A HAPPY LIFE, (Boston and Chicago, [1885])

44. [S]mith, [H]annah [W]hitall, THE UNSELFISHNESS OF GOD AND HOW I DISCOVERED IT (New York, [1903])

45. Steele, Daniel, A SUBSTITUTE FOR HOLINESS; OR, ANTINOMIANISM REVIVED (Chicago and Boston, [1899])

46. Tomlinson, A. J., THE LAST GREAT CONFLICT (Cleveland, 1913)

47. Upham, Thomas C., THE LIFE OF FAITH (Boston, 1845)

48. Washburn, Josephine M., HISTORY AND REMINIS-CENCES OF THE HOLINESS CHURCH WORK IN SOUTH-ERN CALIFORNIA AND ARIZONA (South Pasadena, [1912?])